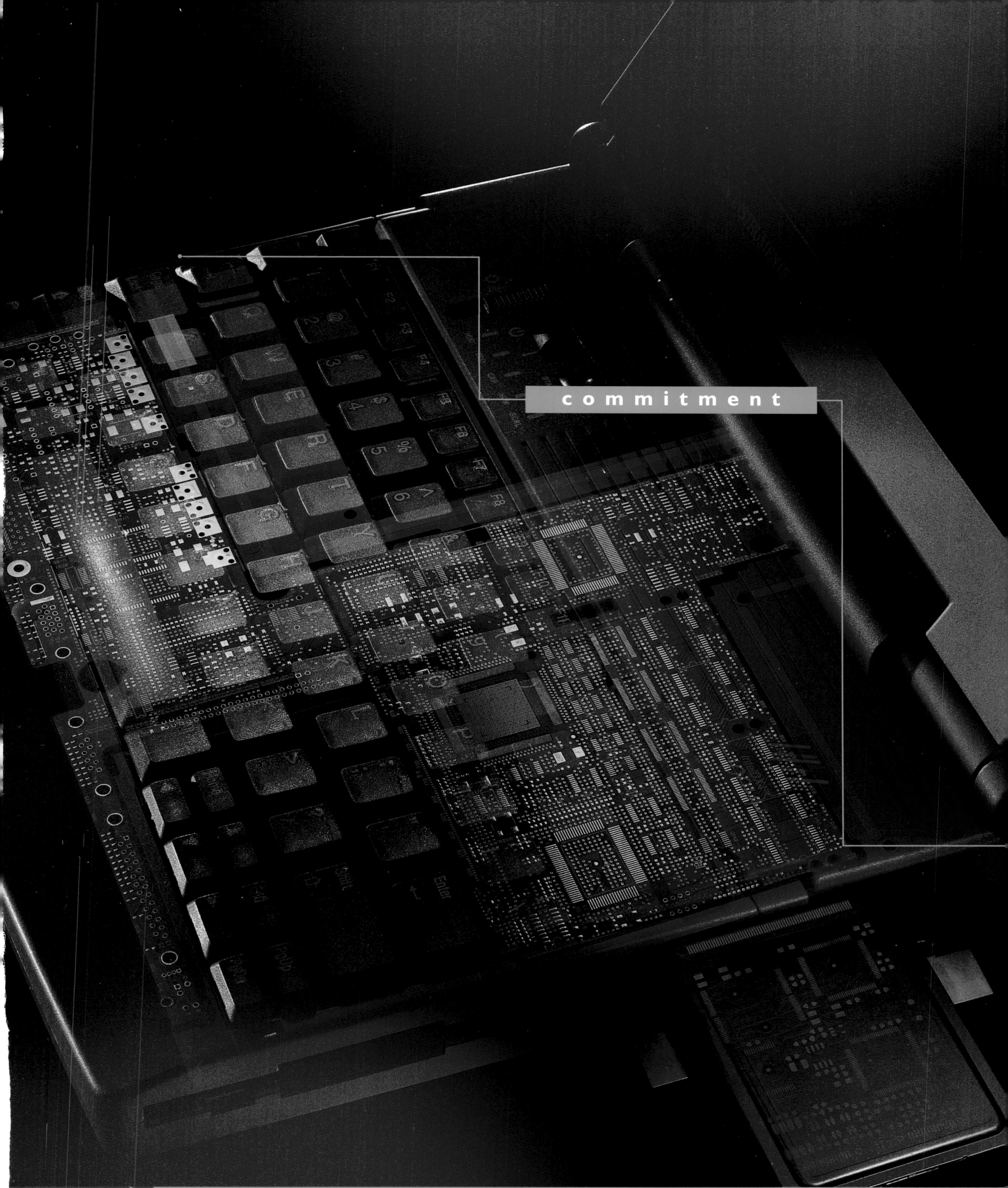

commitment

CONTINENTAL
CIRCUITS
CORP

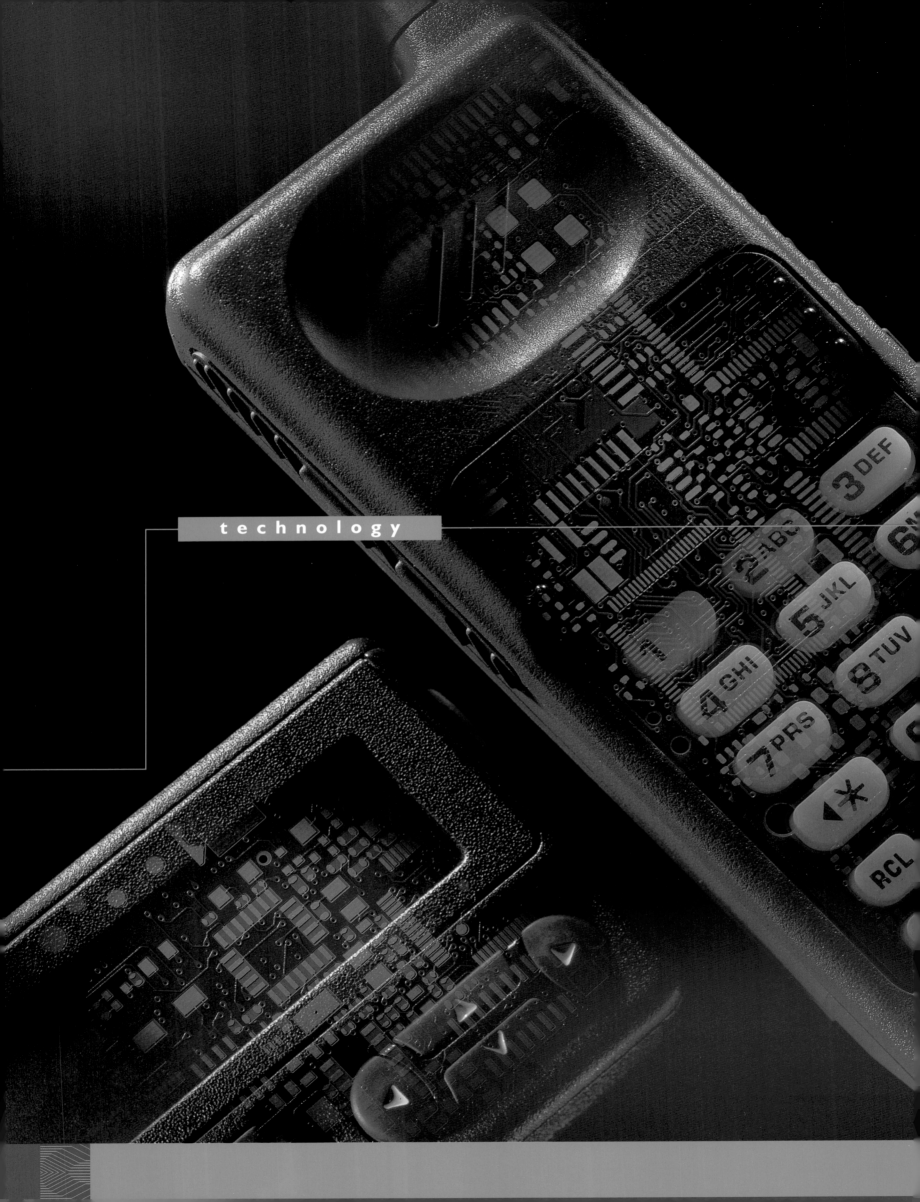

technology

people

objective

Continental Circuits Corp. manufactures complex multilayer, surface-mount circuit boards used in the rapidly growing computer and industrial markets. Continental provides circuit boards for many products including notebook computers, workstations, pagers, cellular phones, network products and servers.

The microprocessor is the "engine" and the circuit board is the transmission, drive train and wheels connecting all of the components delivering a finished product. Evolving technology requires an investment in equipment and facilities, processes, and most importantly—people.

CONTINENTAL CIRCUITS CORP

3502 east roeser road phoenix, arizona 85040

ph 602.268.3461 fax 602.268.0208 net contcirc.com

Greater
PHOENIX

by

Michel F. Sarda

Contributing Photographers

Ken Akers
Timothy Fuller
Kerrick James
Jeff Kida
Mike Moore
Phoenix Photographic
Rick Raymond
Mike Scully
Jerry Sieve
David Smith

Bridgewood Press
Phoenix, Arizona

Acknowledgments

To Ioanna Morfessis, Joyce Haver, Bruce Sankey, Laurie Leach, Duriye Luckett,
and to the entire staff of the **Greater Phoenix Economic Council**, for their support.

For their personal contributions: Gerald W. Alston, Kamal Amin, Bill Ensign, David Ira Goldstein,
Dr. Roy Herberger, Diane Howell, Warren Iliff, John Junker, Bruce Sankey, Beth Schermer,
Bruce Snyder, Joan Squires.

For their friendly contribution and/or appearance: Philip C. Curtis, James DeMars, Donna Fleischer,
Isabelle Hallier, Barbara and Sterling Ridge, Alberto Rios, Fritz Scholder, Paolo Soleri, John Waddell.

For their contribution of photographic materials: Arizona Theater Company, City of Peoria,
Fiesta Bowl, The Phoenix Suns, The Phoenix Symphony.

For their support and for their dedication to the Greater Phoenix community:

America West Airlines
American Graduate School of Int'l Management
Bank of America
Best Western International
Bull HN Information Systems
Cannon & Wendt
Century 21 of the Southwest
CIGNA Healthcare of Arizona
Continental Circuits
Corporate Jets
Dial Corp
Ecosys Biotechnology
Fennemore Craig
Finova
First Interstate Bank
Forever Living Products
Fox Animation Studios

Franchise Finance Corporation of America
Gila River Indian Casino
Gila River Indian Community
Hardaway Marketing Services
Intel
Jennings Strouss & Salmon
Lewis & Roca
McDonnell Douglas Helicopter Systems
Molina Fine Jewelers
Norwest Bank
Sky Harbor International Airport
SunCor Development Company
The Perimeter Center
The Phoenix Suns
United Van Lines/Horizon Moving Systems
WestWorld Of Scottsdale

Grateful acknowledgment for use of the following quotations:
P. 86, Stan Adler; p. 70, 91, Harry Behn; p. 20, Patricia Benton; p. 22, D. Maitland Bushby;
p. 101, Ann Nolan Clark; p. 33, Badger Clark; p. 42, Charles S. Colley; p. 68, Maynard Dixon;
p. 102, Morton H. Fleischer p.19, 26, Sharlot M. Hall; p. 76, Robert B. Miller; p. 95, Jack Nicklaus;
p. 37, 82, Charles S. Poling; p. 81, Margaret E. Schevill; p. 23, Delos H. Smalley;
p. 109, Trevor Southey; p. 74, Vesta H. Vandeveer; p. 21, Beulah M. Wadsworth;
p. 67, Eda Lou Walton; p. 73, Hilda F. Wetherill; p.5, 80, Milo Wiltbank.

Our deepest gratitude and admiration to Blair Morton Armstrong
for her remarkable *Arizona Anthem*, Scottsdale: The Mnemosyne Press, 1982,
a collection of Arizona poetry.

We apologize for credits misinterpreted or omitted unintentionally.

Editor   Donnalee R. Sarda
Design   Sarda Resources, Inc.
Translations   French   Sarda Resources, Inc.
                Spanish   Michael J. Flys, Ph.D.
                German   Birgit Zimmermann
                Japanese   Japanese Communications Consultants, Inc.
                Chinese   Jane Kuo, Ph.D.

Library of Congress Catalog Card Number 94-078217
ISBN 0-927015-12-9
Printed in Hong Kong

To Beth, Bruno and Emily

I'd like to live in the kind of a town
   That's building up, not tumbling down.
A hustling, bustling, busy place
   Where there's always things to do.
A town that's run for the good of all,
   And not for just a few.
If I'm to live in the kind of a town
   That's building up, not tumbling down,
I must be the hustling, bustling kind
   That's not afraid to give.
If it's to build the kind of a place
   In which I'd like to live,
For an up and coming, growing town,
   Where real things are done,
Must be made and built by all
   It can't be built by one.

                                    Milo Wiltbank

Contents

	page
Introduction by Michel F. Sarda	7
A Mythical Rebirth, historical summary	9
Map of Greater Phoenix with photo locations	16
Color Plates	
Legacy	18
Community	36
Lifestyle	74
Business	103
Appendices	
Translations	
Index	

Introduction

by Michel F. Sarda

At the end of the 20th century, the trend seems clear: most human inhabitants of planet Earth live or will live in an urban environment. Already, monster cities assemble populations larger than those of entire countries. More people live in Tokyo than in Canada, more live in Mexico City than in the whole of Australia.

As a result of this urban revolution, probably one of the most important phenomenons in the history of humankind, immense changes affect the way most of us live, the way we relate to our time, to others, to ourselves. Amidst the huge conglomerates of buildings, arteries, running people, moving vehicles and roaring noises that characterize the great cities of today, it is up to each of us to find our place, to choose our way. What was called social and family life must be redefined — or reinvented. Thanks to fast and cheap transportation we are not assigned anywhere permanently. The choice of where to spend our life is not dictated anymore by tradition or by an attachment to the land, but by the pursuit of opportunities. Our lifestyle shapes who we are.

When the uncertainties of world politics and those of a global economy combine, the only sure thing we know is that tomorrow will not be like today. The fulfillment of individual expectations becomes a challenging adventure. One improves the odds by choosing a proper place to live, for instance a place where the tidal wave of modern technology irrigates an inspiring natural setting. With opportunities for the body to exercise, for the mind to produce, for the soul to reflect.

I believe that Greater Phoenix is such a place.

(continued)

Phoenix is a fitting name for this metropolis. Rooted in many mythologies, this symbol of reviving splendor applies well to a city born from the desert where other civilizations blossomed in the past. The gods of many ancient cultures may keep a friendly watch on this young community in the making. Gifted individuals have contributed their vision to its early days, others continue today. A proud, restless city, constantly questioning its own identity and the mirror of its dreams: "Am I the most beautiful?" Well, it was recognized the best-managed city in the world [1]. Not too shabby for a one-million-plus city hardly a century-old.

The communities comprising Greater Phoenix are like a family of talented individuals. Each has its own history, its distinctive "look and feel" that even a hurried visitor can perceive when crossing the invisible line that separates Phoenix from Scottsdale, Tempe, Mesa or Glendale. Each of these cities has its personality, its spirit. Collectively, their diversity contributes to making Greater Phoenix unique.
The capital of a border state is a crossroad of cultures. Forty nationalities are represented on the campus of Arizona State University in Tempe. The Phoenix International Sister Cities program was ranked first in the nation in 1994. The age-old Native American and Hispanic heritages create a testing ground for a new balance between tradition and modernity. In many respects, Greater Phoenix illustrates the future of urbanization.

It is the challenge of this book to illustrate the visible and to try to capture the invisible. Longtime residents may not recognize the place where they grew up, others might not find their favorite spot represented. Like all portraits, this one subjectively selects some traits and ignores others for the purpose of a likeness which might only exist in the eyes of the author. This is an impression carefully noted, not a land survey. It is my hope that it will be shared by many.

1. Award granted by the Carl Bertelsmann Foundation, 1993.

A Mythical Rebirth
An Historical Summary

Human settlements in the valley of the Salt River, where Greater Phoenix is located, have been traced back to prehistoric times. The abundant though unpredictable waters of the Salt combined with a rich alluvial soil and abundant sunshine to support agriculture and to provide for successful harvests. Sedentary, ingenious and peaceful people lived here for thousands of years. Little was left of their passage.

From A.D. 300 to 1400, the Hohokam people (from a Pima word meaning "those who have vanished") occupied the site. They created an elaborate system of canals to bring the whimsical Salt into their fields, sometimes several miles from the river bed. Their remarkable civilization reached its zenith around A.D. 1100, with a network a cities that might have represented up to 100,000 souls — the largest in the early history of North America outside of Mexico. Three centuries later, for reasons that are still obscure — a lasting drought, a lethal epidemic or hostile invaders — they disappeared from the land. Although other Indian tribes were established in the vicinity, the future site of Greater Phoenix remained mostly undisturbed for another 400 years.

In the meantime, the Spanish explored the area, founded and developed Santa Fe and Tucson. The most notable contribution of the new Hispanic order in Arizona came from Father Eusebio Kino. A man of God, this Italian Jesuit was assigned in 1687 to "Pimeria Alta" or Pima territory, a region of New Spain encompassing the north of the present Mexican state of Sonora and the southern part of present-day Arizona. To the peaceful Pimas, as noted by Herbert Bolton, Kino was "the Great White Father. They loved him, and he loved them." [1] Within the 25 years of his presence, Kino built 29 missions, developed farming and ranching, worked as a cartographer and an astronomer. He died in 1711 at the age of sixty-six, "with extreme humility and poverty, as he had lived" wrote Father de Campos, one of his companions. The work of this man of knowledge and compassion was brutally undone in 1767 when the King of Spain expelled the Jesuits from all parts of the Spanish empire. The missions he had created were destroyed by Apache marauders. Today, the statue of Father Kino on horseback faces the Arizona Capitol in Phoenix.

The land was acquired by the United States in 1848, following the Mexican War. There was little in the Salt River valley to attract fur trappers or farmers — not to mention the presence of the dreaded Tonto Apaches. In 1863, after mineral resources of strategic interest were discovered, Arizona was made a territory of the Union. In 1865, at the end of the Civil War, when the Army established Fort McDowell at the eastern end of the valley to protect several mining settlements, the site was essentially a desert.

The creation of this small army post started an unstoppable chain of events. Soon the fort faced difficulties to raise food for the soldiers and for their horses. Residents of the mining communities experienced the same problem. The demand for food and hay, for which the army and the miners were ready to pay a high price, triggered the revival of the Salt River valley.

Here appears an unlikely hero: Jack Swilling, an adventurer from South Carolina, arrived in Arizona in 1857. First a Confederate soldier and deserter, then a freighter and a scout for the Union, he does not match the profile of a major city's founding father. However, he is the one who recognized the presence of the canals dug by the Hohokam, understood their potential, and decided to put them back to work.

Lawrence C. Powell describes Jack Swilling as follows:

He was a man aware of the land's lay and the wind's direction. He saw that the ancient farmers had chanelled water to the drier reaches. Vestiges of their ditches were still visible. Swilling knew naught of the Hohokam. He knew only what he needed to know: that when watered, the sun-baked soil would yield crops; and furthermore that the United States Army paid cash for barley and would provide a market for other crops." [2]

From mining tycoon Henry Wickenburg and others, Swilling received financial support to establish in 1867 the Swilling Irrigating & Canal Company. He followed the ancient plan of the Hohokam, digging north and west from what is today the intersection of 44th and Washington streets. After securing contracts with Fort McDowell and several mining towns, he settled thirty farmers along the new canals. He established himself and his new wife, Trinidad, in the vicinity. Three years later, farmers numbered more than 200 and the cultivated lands had expanded to 1,500 acres.

The naming of Phoenix is owed unequivocally to Darrell Duppa, an English adventurer with a cosmopolitan background, who had conferred upon himself the title of lord. He came to Arizona in 1862 to manage family interests in mining, then started prospecting for himself and warring Indians. At this juncture he probably met with Swilling, later to become his partner in his irrigation company.

When the time came to give the new settlement a name (if only to tell suppliers where to send their goods), suggestions were made, Pumpkinsville, and Salina (from Salt River) among them. The final decision was made in 1869 during a gathering at Pueblo Grande, the Indian ruin close to Swilling's home, certainly after abundant drinking. According to eye witnesses, Duppa climbed to the top of the ancient wall and proclaimed: "As the mythical phoenix rose reborn from its ashes, so shall a great civilization rise here on the ashes of a past civilization. I name thee Phoenix!" All present agreed.

In 1870, the creation of the newly organized Maricopa County marked the beginning of Swilling's fall. The seat of the new county was not located on his property as he wished, but further east, on land not yet appropriated and safe from floods. Swilling took it personnally. His violent nature, aggravated by his abuse of alcohol and drugs, pushed him to move north to Agua Fria, then to gradually step outside the law. Indicted for the holdup of a stagecoach, he was sent to jail in Yuma, where he died in 1878 at the age of forty-eight .
Darrell Duppa had followed his friend to Agua Fria. He later ran a stage station, then sank into alcoholism. He died of pneumonia in 1892.

The early departure of the city's founder did not leave Phoenix without promoters. John T. Alsop became Phoenix' first mayor in 1881 after contributing his authority to its early growth; John "Yours Truly" Smith, a former Union Army officer who negotiated the first contracts with the Army, contributed to moving the territorial capital from Prescott to Phoenix in 1889. These pioneers had come to stay and succeed. Out of hard labor, they established the foundation on which Phoenix would rise. The Arizona Canal, serving the high grounds in the northern part of the valley, a project more ambitious than anything the Hohokam had conceived, was completed in 1885 by an Illinois entrepreneur, William J. Murphy. The Southern Pacific Railroad reached Phoenix and Tempe in 1887. Growth was steady. Maricopa County counted 10,000 residents in 1890, 20,000 at the turn of the century, and 35,000 in 1910.

The catastrophic floods of the Salt River soon appeared to be a major obstacle to the development of the area. Under the leadership of Benjamin A. Fowler, a native of Massachusetts who had moved to Arizona for his health, the Salt River Valley Water Users' Association was created in 1903. With the personal support of President Theodore Roosevelt, who enjoyed visiting the West, adequate legislation was crafted that authorized the construction of the Roosevelt Dam, completed in 1911 and still the highest masonry dam in the world. This technological wonder allowed efficient irrigation control. Lawrence C. Powell describes the mastering of the Salt River as "an heroic story of vision, energy and persistence, in which many strong individuals banded together in common cause."2

The availability of irrigated land had attracted farmers and entrepreneurs who established new communities. Charles Trumbull Hayden, an early supplier to Fort McDowell, had built a ferry to cross the Salt. In 1871 he founded a city on the southern bank, and used Duppa's creative mind to name it Tempe, after the mythological residence of the lesser gods on the foothills of Mount Olympus. A visionary civic leader as well as a shrewd businessman, Hayden recognized the importance of education for the future of the area. In 1885, assisted by Samuel Armstrong, he influenced the territorial legislature to select Tempe as the location of a Normal School of Teachers, for which Hayden and others donated a five-acre piece of property. In the 1930s the institution, under the guidance of its president Dr. Grady Gammage, benefited from the New Deal by successfully applying for federal grants. After the war, faced with an enrollment explosion due to the G.I. Bill, the Normal School became the Arizona State College, before receiving full university status in 1958. Arizona State University is now the fifth largest campus in the

United States with an annual enrollment of over 50,000 students. With the student and faculty population representing nearly half of its 150,000 residents, Tempe offers the attractive, unmistakable flavor of a campus town. In 1992, a local poll designated Tempe as the most desirable place to live in Greater Phoenix.

Mesa, eight miles east of Tempe, was founded in 1878 by Mormon farmers, and was incorporated in 1883. The growth of the city was boosted by the construction of the Roosevelt Dam in the early 1900s. Considered as the "Mormon Capital of Arizona", Mesa celebrated in 1928 the completion of the Mormon Temple, an impressive sanctuary which still serves as a center for the Mormon presence in the state. Rapidly becoming the Valley's second largest community after Phoenix, Mesa grew with the state capital and in 1995, with a population of over 300,000, was in competition with Tucson for the status of second largest city in Arizona.

Glendale, in the northeastern part of the Valley, founded in 1892, was promoted by William J. Murphy, developer of the Arizona Canal. Astutely, Murphy had made sure that the railroad would serve his development. Initially populated with Eastern Europe immigrants, Glendale farmers proved to be so resourceful, despite setbacks with attempts to grow sugar beet and cotton, that Glendale was given the name of "Vegetable Capital of the Southwest." Glendale is now the leading town in the west valley, with a population of more than 150,000.

Scottsdale was founded in 1893 by Army chaplain Winfield Scott, a long-time promoter of immigration. Scott had been invited to visit the Phoenix area in 1888 to evaluate its potential. Convinced by what he saw, he purchased 640 acres of land that are now the center of Scottsdale. He settled on his property after retiring from the army in 1893, and introduced citrus growing. His charisma and his moral influence as a Baptist preacher soon gave Scottsdale the reputation of a "clean" town. In 1897, when the Anti-Saloon League was formed, it might have deterred the rugged pioneers of the West, because the growth of the city remained among the slowest in the Valley. There were no more than a hundred residents at the turn of the century, and only a thousand in 1940. In the meantime, Scottsdale had acquired a specific identity as a friendly community for artists and health seekers, attracting creators of the caliber of architect Frank Lloyd Wright and painter Philip Curtis. The benefit of this image-building effort came later, with a huge dividend. From a population of 10,000 in 1960, Scottsdale exploded as a cultural and tourism mecca that led to its designation as the "Most Livable City" in the United States in 1993. In 1995, with more than 150,000 residents and one of the largest incorporated area in the nation, encompassing desert and mountain ranges, Scottsdale experiences the pressure of exhilarating growth.

Dr. Alexander Chandler, a veterinarian from Detroit, came to the Valley in 1887. Along with eastern investors, he purchased large tracts of land south of Mesa and started his own irrigation company. After Roosevelt Dam was completed and the federal government had acquired the entire canal system as part of the project, Dr. Chandler founded the town bearing his name in 1912 by subdividing his 18,000-acre ranch. He had in mind a model city, the "Pasadena of Arizona" and promoted it nationwide. The San Marcos resort rapidly became a popular winter destination for wealthy businessmen. In the late 1920s, Chandler interested Frank Lloyd Wright, who was participating in the design of the Arizona Biltmore, in planning the city of his dreams. The Great Depression, which severely affected the young town, put an early end to this project.

Times changed, and Chandler grew with the rest of the area. Chandler is home to Intel's giant microchip production plant, among many other high-tech industries.

Other agricultural settlements followed the extension of the irrigation canal system. Peoria was established in 1888 by friends of William J. Murphy. Buckeye was created in 1889, Tolleson in 1910 and Gilbert two years later.

Statehood was granted to Arizona in 1912 and Phoenix benefited from its status as state capital. By the end of the 1920s, the local economy was still essentially based on agriculture, although tourists were already a contributing factor. Manufacturing industries were noticeably absent.

At the bottom of the Great Depression, came a man of vision, who would play an essential role in the development of the area: Walter Reed Bimson, a banker from Denver, educated in Chicago and Harvard. As vice-president of the Harris Trust & Savings Bank of Chicago, he had several occasions to visit Arizona to survey the production of cotton. After Harris Trust showed little interest in a more customer-oriented banking policy, Bimson accepted to head the Valley National Bank in Phoenix. Only days after his arrival in December, 1932 after the closure of all California banks, Bimson's decisive intervention in convincing Governor Moeur to close the banks of Arizona before their assets could be swept away to California saved the state from financial disaster. Later, Bimson put his then-innovative "Lend money!" philosophy to work, helping Phoenix to recover from the Depression and to attract large manufacturers such as Motorola. He also set new standards in community involvement, contributing to the creation of the Phoenix Art Museum and of the Phoenix Symphony after the war.

Bradford Luckingham describes this period of history:

"By 1940, the urban framework of the Valley of the Sun was well established. The agricultural capital of the Southwest and the home of the capital of Arizona, the area functioned as an economic, political and social focal point in the region. A national tourist attraction, it was linked to the rest of the country by road, rail and air transportation networks. During the 1930s, a strong relationship evolved between the federal government and the desert urban center, and New Deal programs helped especially to alleviate problems that surfaced. The Great Depression retarded progress, but in the future that relationship between Washington and the Phoenix area would grow stronger and the metropolitan complex would eventually develop to proportions undreamed of in the past, with the city of Phoenix continuing as its vital hub and dominant force. An economic boom and a population explosion during and after World War II would quickly push Phoenix toward metropolis status." [3]

In 1940, because of the development of the war in Europe, and after observing the importance of air warfare, the federal government had decided to create new air bases for pilot training. Arizona was allocated six facilities, five of which were in Greater Phoenix: Luke and Williams, Falcon field and Thunderbird 1 and 2. After the attack on Pearl Harbor, the West Coast was perceived as vulnerable, and inland locations were preferred for war industries. Arizona offered perfect weather conditions and vast inhabited areas for gunnery range. With the active support of Senators Ernest W. McFarland and Carl T. Hayden (son of the Tempe founder), and with the favorable business environment created locally by individuals such as Walter Bimson, aviation and high-technology set foot in the Valley of the Sun.

Among the first industries to come to the area was the Goodyear Aircraft Corporation. Paul W. Litchfield, head of the company, had already contributed to the creation of Litchfield Park and the Wigwam Resort. Others followed, such as Alcoa, AiResearch (Garrett) and Sperry Rand. The vast number of troops transiting through the Valley generated a need for new services. By the end of the war, Luke Air Force Base was the world's largest advanced flying training school, and still is. From a population of 65,000 in 1940, Phoenix grew to 106,000 in 1950. Maricopa County grew similarly from 186,000 to 331,000.

Still, the real boom was yet to come. The postwar development of air conditioning changed not only the way of life in the Valley, but industry production schedules. Hundreds of manufacturing enterprises opened their doors or relocated to the area. As an example, there was more construction in Phoenix during the year 1959 than during the entire period from 1914 to 1946. The same year, in application of an aggressive annexation program, Phoenix more than doubled in area and gained 100,000 new residents. Rapidly becoming a major distribution center for the entire Southwest, Phoenix saw its population jump to 440,000 in 1960, a 311% progression in ten years, the highest rate in the nation.

The presence of industry leaders in advanced electronics (Motorola, Intel, Honeywell, Bull HN, Digital, GTE, to name a few) and aerospace (McDonnell Douglas Helicopters, Garrett, B.F.Goodrich, among many others) has promoted Greater Phoenix to its status as a major high-tech center. Tourism has generated the apparition of a number of destination hotels and resorts such as the Phoenician, the Scottsdale Princess, the Boulders, that regularly appear at the top of national ratings. Healthcare has become a major industry, with facilities such as the Neurological Barrows Institute and the Mayo Clinic Scottsdale. Recent prominence in sports and culture is a sign that a new level of urban quality has been reached.

This phenomenal growth is still going on. The combination of fine weather, superb natural environment, affordable land and housing and great lifestyle is more attractive than ever. The people moving to Greater Phoenix are not farmers any more. Yet perhaps the pioneer spirit is still with them, as many are entrepreneurs and creators from around the nation and beyond, attracted by the opportunities offered by a fast-growing, innovative community. Others come and stay for the magnificent natural setting, the sunny days and the casual lifestyle. Maricopa County, which houses the cities of Greater Phoenix, passed the 2-million mark in the late 1980s. From capital of the Southwest, Greater Phoenix is becoming the capital of the Sunbelt.

Notes:
1. Crutchfield, James A. *It Happened in Arizona.* Helena, MT: Falcon Press Publishing Co., 1994.
2. Powell, Lawrence Clark. *Arizona.* Albuquerque: University of New Mexico Press, 1990.
3. Luckingham, Bradford. *Phoenix, the history of a southwestern metropolis.* Tucson: the University of Arizona Press, 1989.

Bell Rd.

To Sedona & Flagstaff

Surprise

El Mirage

57

58

Litchfield Rd.

Peoria

53

Grand Ave.

Interstate 17

Olive Ave.

Dunlap Ave.

Northern Ave.

Glendale Ave.

Glendale 48

Luke Air Force Base

Camelback Rd.

91 Indian School Rd.

Litchfield Park Thomas Rd.

Interstate 10

To Los Angeles

Van Buren St. 25

Buckeye **Avondale**

Buckeye Rd.

19th Ave

Goodyear

91st Ave

Baseline Rd.

36

South Mountain

THE COMMUNITIES OF THE
GREATER PHOENIX ECONOMIC COUNCIL
(Ranked by Population)

Phoenix — The eighth largest city in the nation, Phoenix is the hub of the rapidly growing southwestern United States. It is situated in Maricopa County and is the capital of the State of Arizona. The name Phoenix, symbolizing rebirth, was chosen because the city was built on the remains of the ancient Hohokam Indian civilization, whose farmers laid out the irrigation canals still in use today. Phoenix has a well-diversified economic base, manufacturing being the leading employer, followed by the tourism and hospitality industries.

Mesa — Spanish for "tabletop," Mesa was so named because it sits atop a plateau overlooking the Valley that surrounds Greater Phoenix. Mesa, Arizona's third largest city, is among the fastest growing communities in the nation. It is located 12 miles southeast of Phoenix. With its own "downtown" and suburban residential settings, Mesa offers many of the advantages of big city living while retaining the best aspects of community life.

Glendale — One of the fastest-growing communities in Greater Phoenix, Glendale ranks as Arizona's fourth largest city. The recent population increase is largely due to affordable quality homes, excellent educational institutions, including the world-renowned American "Thunderbird" Graduate School for International Management and Midwestern University, and enjoyable recreational amenities. Manufacturing, service sector and military activities comprise a large portion of the economic base.

Tempe — has developed from a small college town and bedroom community into a full-fledged city with a strong, diversified economy. It is home to Arizona State University. Both are fifth largest — that is, Tempe is the fifth largest city in the State; and ASU is the fifth largest university in the nation. Known for its highly educated populace, Tempe is a sophisticated city and center for learning, culture and technology. Old Town Tempe has a charm all its own.

Scottsdale — This urbane, sophisticated and cultured western city has sprung from a tiny citrus farming cluster of hardly 2,000 persons in 1951. Scottsdale's lifestyle includes well-planned living, working and shopping spaces. The city is known for its architectural and landscape design excellence, and for rich cultural experiences (museums, art galleries and performing arts abound) and for planned business and recreational environments, including the finest golf courses and several five-star resorts.

Chandler — Located 20 miles southeast of Phoenix, Chandler was once a quiet farm town centered around a tree-lined plaza. More recently, it has become recognized as a center for high-tech industry and business. As such, it is a city on the move, now ranked as one of the fastest growing cities in the country. The Chandler Center for the Performing Arts draws crowds to its events from miles away.

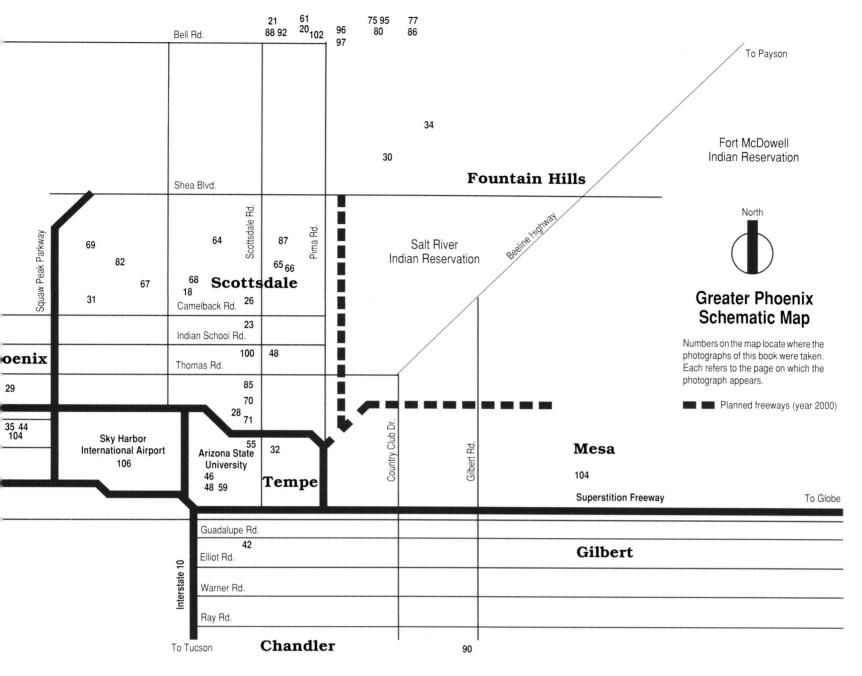

Greater Phoenix Schematic Map

Numbers on the map locate where the photographs of this book were taken. Each refers to the page on which the photograph appears.

■ ■ ■ Planned freeways (year 2000)

Peoria — is a fast-growing suburban community in the northwest portion of the Valley. Formerly an agricultural town, Peoria is today a comfortable bedroom community with a friendly small town atmosphere. At its Peoria Sports Complex, the Seattle Mariners and the San Diego Padres Baseball teams hold spring training.

Gilbert — In the southeast corner of Maricopa County, Gilbert is within a half-hour drive from downtown Phoenix. Its population boom as an Arizona community is largely due to the quality of life residents enjoy. A superior school system, quality housing, recreational amenities and employment opportunities are some of the reasons that new residents and businesses are attracted here.

Avondale — is a bustling residential community in the rapidly growing West Valley region of Maricopa County. Just 15 miles to the west of Phoenix, Avondale is undergoing a transition from an agricultural economy to one based on light industry and commercial enterprises.

Fountain Hills — This planned, family-oriented community was established in 1970. Before that date, the area was a cattle ranch, part of one of the largest land and cattle holdings in Arizona. The centerpiece of Fountain Hills is the world's tallest man-made fountain, a focal point that attracts thousands of visitors and residents each year. The scenic views from many vantage points in Fountain Hills are breathtaking.

Surprise — is located in the fast-growing northwest part of the Valley. This once sleepy little farm town has awakened to new business and residential opportunities. The exceptional expansion of a planned transportation system places Surprise in the path of progress and offers businesses and industries golden advantages.

Goodyear — is a suburban community, 17 miles from Phoenix to the west. The town name comes from the Goodyear Tire and Rubber Company which began cotton farming here in 1916. Goodyear has a strong economic base and is poised for expansion throughout the end of this century and into the next.

Buckeye — At the confluence of the Gila and Hassayampa Rivers, thirty miles west of Phoenix, the town of Buckeye was founded in 1888. It prides itself on a quality lifestyle and family-centered environment. In its three generations, Buckeye citizens have withstood floods and drought and managed to transform the desert land into a garden and productive valley.

Litchfield Park — This planned residential community, 16 miles west of Phoenix, boasts a small town atmosphere and casual lifestyle, all in a unique suburban setting. It's the home of The Wigwam, one of Arizona's superb five-star resorts.

El Mirage — is a stable residential community, 16 miles northwest of Phoenix. Traditionally, El Mirage has been a farm community, but is now developing its economic potential while maintaining its pleasant small town environment.

Legacy

The magic of dawn on Camelback Mountain recalls that this was a sacred site to the ancient inhabitants.

(photo Jerry Sieve/Adstock)

Silent the new land waited,
Far from the roads of life,
Where men set face in an age-long race,
And strive in an age-long strife...
Here was peace in the stillness,
Here was joy in the sun;
And freedom and right not born of might,
Nor of wars hard-lost, or won.

Sharlot M. Hall

Yet joyous flowers bloom
As if the womb of earth
Clasped in such secret spell
This touch of loveliness.

Patricia Benton

The Sonoran desert that surrounds Greater Phoenix extends south into Mexico. The blooming of a city, now among the ten largest in the United States, in such an environment results from complex historical and economical factors. It is best symbolized by the delicate flowers that, every spring, grace the "prickly pear" cactus.

(photo Michel F. Sarda)

20

Farewell, men of mystery
Wise men lost to history.

Beulah M. Wadsworth

Human dwellings along the Salt and the Verde rivers have been traced back thousands of years. An elaborate irrigation system was built by the Hohokam (a Papago word meaning *Those who have gone*), an elusive civilization that mysteriously vanished 800 years ago. Native American cultures permeate many aspects of Arizona life. Art is one of the most visible. "Incantation", a lifesize bronze sculpture by Arizona artist Buck McCain is a "tribute to the inner strength, perseverance and faith comprising every man".

(photo Michel F. Sarda)

The years have passed but men will not forget
Their debt to you, though ages lie between
Your time and theirs, but rather voice regret
Because they knew you not. Your soul shall glean
A harvest born of happiness, for you
Have sown far better than you dreamed or knew.

D. Maitland Bushby — *Lines for Father Kino*

An explorer, a cartographer, a rancher, and a man of God, Jesuit Eusebio Kino is a luminous figure of early Arizona. The statue in front of the State Capitol, a work by Julian Martinez of Hermosillo, was offered to Arizona by the Mexican State of Sonora.

(photo Michel F. Sarda)

22

Offer the freedom of their cities fair,
Fountains of youth, distilled in mountain air,
And every beauty 'neath the purple dome
That canopies their loved and chosen home.

Delos H. Smalley

The fountain and the sculpture by Bob Parks, on Fifth Avenue in Scottsdale, illustrate the role played by both horses and water in attracting settlers to this land.

(photo Michel F. Sarda)

Saint Mary's church was made a Basilica by
Pope John-Paul II when he visited Phoenix in
1987. The two elegant towers, built by French
missionaries a century ago, are a popular
landmark in downtown Phoenix.

(photo Michel F. Sarda)

The Capitol building was built after Phoenix became the Arizona territorial capital in 1890. The copper roof symbolizes the contribution of the mining industry to the prosperity of the area. Statehood was granted in 1912. Tradition held that the statue on top of the dome was used for target practice by drunken cowboys. And indeed, when it was removed for restoration in the mid-1970s, it was riddled with bullet holes.

(photo Michel F. Sarda)

Songs and laughter, hopes and dreams,
Sheltered under these roof-beams;
Life and death and love and fear —
Each one had its moment here.
Now those first-come men are gone
And the old house stands alone,
Filled with whispering memories.

Sharlot M. Hall

The Jokake Inn was the former home of artist Jessie Benton Evans. In 1927, it became a resort which rapidly attracted an elegant clientele from all over the United States. The old adobe building is now an intriguing landmark on the grounds of The Phoenician Resort.

(photo Michel F. Sarda)

(above)

The Arizona Historical Society Museum in Papago Park introduces the visitor to various aspects of Arizona history from the past centuries to the present. An ancient alchemist symbol representing the mystical qualities of copper was chosen for the Society's logo.

(opposite page)

The Heard Museum is a favorite destination for Phoenix visitors for its innovative and respectful presentation of Indian American cultures. It was founded in 1929 by Dwight and Maie Heard, initially to house their personal collection of Native American artifacts. *Earth Song*, a sculpture by Allan Houser, was dedicated in 1979.

(photos Michel F. Sarda)

Completed in 1929, based on a design by Frank Lloyd Wright, the Arizona Biltmore Hotel rapidly became — and still is — a prestigious destination, favored by international celebrities and film stars. It was recently restored and expanded.

(photo Michel F. Sarda)

After discovering Arizona in the late 1920s, when he contributed to the design of the Arizona Biltmore Hotel, master architect Frank Lloyd Wright came back in 1937 to establish a winter home, studio and workshop on 600 acres of unspoiled desert he had purchased on the foothills of the McDowell Mountains. Taliesin West, named after his Wisconsin home, was built with indigenous materials. It grew right out of the desert, with which it blends seamlessly.

Until his death in 1959, Frank Lloyd Wright designed and built many original, innovative buildings in the Phoenix area. His legacy is easily recognizable through more recent works by his former associates. Today architects from all over the world come to visit what they consider as one of the sanctuaries of modern architecture. Taliesin West is still an active architectural firm and cultural center, and the winter headquarters for the Frank Lloyd Wright Foundation. It was designated in 1982 as a U.S. landmark.

(photo Michel F. Sarda)

With beauty all around me,
I walk.
With beauty within me,
I walk.

Navajo Chant

Native American students receive recognition from their peers at the Arizona State University annual pow-wow, in an inspirational and colorful homage.

(photo Michel F. Sarda)

When my rope takes hold on a two-year old
By the foot or the neck or the horn
He kin plunge and fight till his eyes go white
But I'll throw him as sure as you're born.

Badger Clark

Ranching remains a major activity in Arizona.
Rodeos perpetuate the spirit of the Old West.

(photo Mike Scully / Adstock)

33

The Valley of the Sun — the name locals give to Greater Phoenix — and its residents have always enjoyed the magnificent Sonoran desert and mountains such as the Santans, Estrella, Camelback and the McDowells.

After rapid urban growth threatened this sensitive environment, citizens came to the realization that the time had come to take action and to protect the beautiful nature that attracted them here in the first place. Groups such as the McDowell Sonoran Land Trust have been formed to raise people's awareness, and to find and implement solutions.

Bill Ensign
President, The McDowell Sonoran Land Trust

With its breathtaking sceneries and distinctive flora, the neighboring desert looks more like a garden than a hostile wilderness. Here are the foothills of the McDowell Mountains.

(photo Michel F. Sarda)

Greater Phoenix is one of the most dynamic urban areas in the country. Exciting new buildings seem to pop out of the ground, and older landmarks receive caring attention. The new Phoenix City Hall blends gently into, and directly communicates with, the renovated Orpheon Theater.

(photo Michel F. Sarda)

Community

I was the wilderness, but now
I am a fruited place,
Yielding my wealth as tribute
To a gallant, regal race.

Charles S. Poling

(opposite page)
From South Mountain, the perspective of
Central Avenue and the downtown Phoenix
skyline showcases urban vitality.

(photo Kerrick James/Adstock)

(above)
The "Puddle Jumpers", by artist Glenna Goodacre, bring a joyful animation to the grounds of the Dial Corp headquarters on Central Avenue. The group could symbolize the communities comprising Greater Phoenix heading for the future with the determination of youth.

(opposite page)
Patriot Square in downtown Phoenix is a setting of choice for a variety of popular events. Here, a multicultural celebration is organized by the Thank You America Foundation.

(photos Michel F. Sarda)

Greater Phoenix owes the diversity of its population to the region being located at a crossroads of traditions and cultures. Also, one of the youngest populations in the United States resides here.

(clockwise from top left)

A participant to the Parada del Sol in Scottsdale, the largest horse-driven parade in existence, heralds designer earrings with her western wear; supporting local sports teams starts at an early age; kids are introduced to the mysteries of the Old West; Hispanic dancers contribute their colorful heritage to the Fiesta Bowl Parade.

(photos Michel F. Sarda)

The emergence of the Phoenix Suns as one of
the premier teams in the National Basketball
Association generates strong—and outwardly
apparent— community support.

41

The Yaquis are Mexican Indians who came to the United States during the Mexican Revolution to earn money to help the cause in their homeland. Many remained to settle two distinctive colonies in Tucson and south of Tempe. The Yaquis are well known for the Pasqua celebrations which are held at the Catholic church in their village each year at Easter.

There are more Indians in Arizona than in any other state in the union. Their varied cultures are a vital part of the interweavings of the cultural tapestry that provides Arizona with its unique heritage.

Dr. Charles C. Colley

In the early 1920s, the Yaquis established the colorful neighborhood of Guadalupe, south of Tempe. Outdoor murals tell stories of cross-cultural sharing and understanding.

(photo Michel F. Sarda)

Every year, the Morning Star festival is an occasion for Native Americans to gather and celebrate their traditions. For the 50th anniversary of the end of World War II, Navajo soldiers pay homage to the legendary "Code Talkers" who successfully challenged the Japanese Intelligence.

(photo Michel F. Sarda)

Great attention in recent years to the quality of urban spaces in downtown Phoenix resulted in national recognition from *Architecture Magazine.*

(from top left, clockwise)

Bronze dancers, part of a 12-figure group by John Waddell, grace The Herberger Theater grounds; highrise buildings are a backdrop for the old Phoenix Court House and City Hall; the new Phoenix City Hall is headquarters for the Carl Bertelsmann Foundation's "Best Managed City in the World"; Heritage Square mixes historical buildings, such as the Victorian era Rosson House — with the contemporary, award-winning Lath House.

(photos Michel F. Sarda)

The gardens and water features of the Arizona Center provide for cool and quiet spaces to enjoy a break in the middle of a busy day.

(photo Michel F. Sarda)

The larger-than-life and welcoming bronze jackrabbits by sculptor Mark Rossi, at Centerpoint on Mill Avenue in Tempe, became an instant landmark when installed in 1993. Young residents quickly "adopted" them.

(photo Michel F. Sarda)

Beautiful weather makes outdoor events a
Greater Phoenix signature. Among several
others, "Sunday on Central" attracts Valley
residents to the very heart of their region.

(photo Michel F. Sarda)

Communities comprising Greater Phoenix show a great vitality in building innovative and inviting public spaces and amenities.

(from top left, clockwise)

The popular Centerpoint on Mill Avenue in Tempe is a meeting place for students of nearby Arizona State University; Glendale's City Hall includes an outdoor theater; the new Scottsdale Public Library caters to a highly educated clientele; Tempe's City Hall, with its reverse pyramid shape, also serves as a landmark and a conversation piece.

(photos Michel F. Sarda)

48

(above)
The large student population in Tempe has chosen Hayden Square as a location for gatherings, dining and entertainment.
(photo Michel F. Sarda)

(overleaf)
The success of the Phoenix Suns in the National Basketball Association has contributed to building strong community support. Here, the Phoenix Suns battle the Houston Rockets at America West Arena.

(photo courtesy of the Phoenix Suns)

49

Because of its mild weather most of the year, Greater Phoenix has emerged as a sports center of national stature. Major sports events take place during winter and early spring. The Cactus League brings several Major League Baseball teams to the Valley for spring training. These teams have developed a friendly relationship with their community of adoption. Here, the California Angels participate in the Fiesta Bowl Parade.

(photo Michel F. Sarda)

State-of-the-art sports facilities can be found in most towns of the Valley of the Sun. Peoria's Sports Complex attracts the San Diego Padres and the Seattle Mariners for their seasonal training.

(photo Phoenix Photographic)

53

Following the initial Fiesta Bowl game in 1971, Arizona Governor Jack Williams looked into his crystal ball and stated: "We have every confidence that the caliber of this great sports event will be heightened even more in the years to come."

To think that over 20 years later, the Fiesta Bowl has grown to be one of America's top bowl games; to think that the Fiesta Bowl festival consisted of 10 events in 1971 and now stages 60 year-round events; to think that the Fiesta Bowl Parade is Arizona's largest one-day spectator event, attracting over 300,000 street spectators; one has to wonder if Williams ever imagined this much success.

It was all merely an idea in 1968, when former ASU president G. Homer Durham mentioned the plan at an awards banquet. But with the hard work and determination of thousands of Arizona volunteers, the Fiesta Bowl has climbed to the top, and continues to follow its initial guiding principle: the Fiesta Bowl will develop a multi-event festival that will revolve around one of the nation's top collegiate bowl games.

John Junker
Fiesta Bowl Executive Director

At the turn of every New Year, the Fiesta Bowl Parade, Marching Band Contest and football game attract thousands of residents and visitors to colorful, exhilarating events.

(photos Michel F. Sarda)

Arizona State University football is an institution in Tempe and the Valley of the Sun. It is the oldest sports entity in the Valley and thousands of alumni and fans support the program.

ASU is nationally known for its gridiron success. Names like Danny White, David Fulcher, John Jefferson, Mike Haynes, Charley Taylor, Woody Green, Al Harris and J.D. Hill roll off the tongue of sports fans everywhere. To date, almost 12 million fans have watched the Sun Devils play football in Sun Devil Stadium alone.

Bruce Snyder
Head Football Coach, Arizona State University

Arizona State University's impressive Sun Devil Stadium reflects the pride of this institution for its outstanding achievements in sports. The 75,000-seat stadium, home to the Arizona Cardinals, was selected for the 1996 NFL Super Bowl game.

(photo Jeff Kida, courtesy of Fiesta Bowl)

I am not an Athenian or a Greek, but a citizen of the world.
Socrates

"Thunderbird", The American Graduate School of International Management is an important resource for American businesses. Known worldwide for its Master of International Management program, Thunderbird is also widely known for its executive education program. It also provides open-enrollment courses and customized programs. Businesses can also get help through Thunderbird class projects, faculty consulting and internships. As a Center of International Business Education and Research, Thunderbird has created several centers and institutes to help businesses with specific international concerns, such as the NAFTA Center and the International Business Ethics Institute. The School also has a government-funded program to help American firms explore trade and investment opportunities in the emerging Russian market.

Dr. Roy A. Herberger, Jr., President

(opposite page)
The new Phoenix Central Public Library made headlines in architectural magazines as one of the most innovative facilities in the nation. Designed by Arizona architect Will Bruder, it combines high-tech looks with sophisticated details, such as the circular skylights inspired by Labrouste's Bibliothèque Nationale in Paris.

(photo Michel F. Sarda)

Greater Phoenix offers an outstanding choice of educational facilities of the highest standards. Besides the innovative Maricopa Community Colleges referred to nationally as an example of excellence and efficiency, Arizona State University, now the fifth largest university in the country with 50,000 students representing more than 40 nationalities, ranks among the highest in many fields.

(clockwise from top left)

The new campus of ASU West; Sterling Ridge, former State Representative and former Mayor of Glendale initiated, with his wife Barbara, ASU West; Hayden Library at ASU features a sunken courtyard to enjoy the Arizona weather while studying; the Nelson Fine Arts Center at ASU, designed by world-known architect Antoine Predock, is a rehearsal place of choice for a student of the nearby School of Music.

(photos Michel F. Sarda)

On a warm May afternoon of 1957, Frank Lloyd Wright and ASU President Grady Gammage walked the length and breadth of the campus, seeking a site for a university auditorium. Mr. Wright studied the grassy acreage of the women's athletic field in the southwest corner of the campus and, noting its circular frontage, declared: "I believe this is the site. The structure should be circular in design, with outstretching arms saying 'welcome to Arizona'."
In the same year, Mr. Wright traveled to Bagdad to meet with King Faisal and other Iraqi officials for initial consultations on a cultural center, one of whose main components was an opera house. Preliminary drawings were prepared over the next months. However, due to the overthrow in 1958 of the Iraqi government and the assassination of the king, the project was abandoned. It was disarmingly sensible to transpose the Bagdad opera house to another desert environment – the Sonoran desert in Arizona.
Neither Mr. Wright nor Dr. Gammage lived to see their dream materialize. However, the Arizona legislature voted funds for the structure in its 1961 session and the Board of Regents approved President Homer Durham's recommendation that the building be named, "The Grady Gammage Memorial Auditorium."
Among the events at the September, 1964 dedication ceremonies, Eugene Ormandy conducted the Philadelphia Philharmonic Orchestra in the hall's first performance. Along with Beethoven's Ninth Symphony, the orchestra appropriately played Richard Strauss's "A Hero's Life." After the applause had died down, Mr. Ormandy returned to the podium and said to a hushed audience: "This is not only the most beautiful room I have ever played in, but acoustically it is the finest I have ever experienced."

Kamal Amin
Architect and Structural Engineer
Former member of the Frank Lloyd Wright design team
for the Grady Gammage Memorial Auditorium

(photo Michel F. Sarda)

59

THE GREATER INDOORS

There's no denying the great outdoors is a major attraction of Greater Phoenix. The sun shines 86 percent of the year, a fact that practically challenges residents to enjoy the region's superb golf and tennis facilities. But recreation is just one of the many entertainment options available in Greater Phoenix. The region's impressive artistic and cultural activities have long had residents trading in their casual wear for black-tie attire. Spacious and stylish performing arts centers provide accommodations for the region's own symphony orchestras and theaters, opera, ballet and dance companies. Original plays are produced on a regular basis.

Gammage Auditorium on the Tempe campus of Arizona State University is a frequent host for touring productions of hit Broadway plays, as is Phoenix Symphony Hall in downtown Phoenix. The Herberger Theater Center is a perfect site for dance and theatrical productions. ASU, Blockbuster Desert Sky Pavilion and many other venues throughout the region attract the world's biggest musical stars. More than 20 museums — including the Phoenix Art Museum, the Heard Museum, the Museum of Science & Technology and the Mesa Southwest Museum — and dozens of art galleries, bring art and history to the forefront. The region's Native American and Hispanic heritage is embraced with a year-round schedule of events.

Arts and crafts are the major attraction at many outdoor festivals which attract hundreds of thousands of people in a single weekend. The Old Town Tempe Festival of the Arts is one example of this phenomenon; Chandler's Ostrich Festival is another.

The arts have found an audience in Greater Phoenix, and they will continue to play a prominent role in the economy and lifestyle.

All things around me are restored in beauty.

Navajo Chant

Art collectors Donna and Morton Fleischer have contributed a new museum dedicated to California impressionists. As Museum director, Donna Fleischer often guides visitors through the exquisitely-designed space.

(photo Michel F. Sarda)

61

Since its first season in 1947, The Phoenix Symphony has become Arizona's largest performing arts organization and has earned international recognition. In 1982, The Phoenix Symphony became the state's only full-time, professional orchestra, attracting and retaining virtuoso-level musicians. Internationally renowned guest artists regularly appear with the symphony.

The orchestra performs more than 160 concerts annually throughout the state. Programs range from classical, chamber and pops to concerts designed specifically for families and children. In addition, The Phoenix Symphony performs for approximately 65,000 students each year in outreach programs, often in the schools.

Joan H. Squires
President and CEO, The Phoenix Symphony

(clockwise from top left)
James DeMars, composer (left), and Alberto Rios, poet, both with faculty positions at ASU, have each received national recognition; art by sculptor Pat Mathiesen at the Esplanade; a production of Gisele by Ballet Arizona; members of The Phoenix Symphony.

(photos by Michel F. Sarda / Ballet Arizona / Rick Raymond)

The arts are one of the most important meeting grounds for any city. They provide places where a community can come together to learn more about themselves and others. Phoenix is truly blessed with an ever expanding, ever improving cultural scene. On any given day there are dozens of choices for high quality exposure to the arts for everyone from the youngest to the oldest residents.

Arizona Theatre Company, the State Theatre of Arizona, draws to downtown Phoenix thousands of Phoenicians each week to enjoy the highest quality plays performed by top-notch professionals in the beautiful Herberger Theater Center. With our mainstage programming, as well as our many outreach programs into the community, ATC hopes to open windows on the ideas that make us one community and celebrate the differences that give the Southwest such a rich diversity.

David Ira Goldstein
Artistic Director, Arizona Theatre Company

A scene of the extraordinary production of
Dracula by the Arizona Theatre Company.

(photo Timothy Fuller, courtesy of ATC)

Fate awaits as I turn horror into art and mask my face with fake serenity.
Fritz Scholder

Arizona's unique lifestyle and the splendor of its natural outdoors attract some of the greatest artistic talents of our time.

(above)

Visionary, world-known architect Paolo Soleri welcomes young visitors to the poetic setting of his Cosanti Foundation in Scottsdale. The model in the background is one illustration of the concept of arcology — the satisfaction of human housing needs in the respect of nature — that Soleri has relentlessly promoted for more than thirty years.

(opposite page)

Fritz Scholder in his studio in Scottsdale. Scholder's paintings, sculptures and publications have reached international acclaim with their combination of haunting and meaningful subjects, masterfully crafted.

(photos Michel F. Sarda)

In the house of long life
I will wander
In the house of happiness
I will wander

Navajo Chant

Philip C. Curtis was among the first artists to settle in Arizona. His meticulous technique serves a sensitive, surrealistic vision of the world that combines poetry, nostalgia and humor.

(photo Michel F. Sarda)

I walk with the gods;
Gods go before me,
Gods follow after me,
I walk in the middle.

Eda Lou Walton

John Waddell's bronze figures can be seen
in many homes and public places of Greater
Phoenix. Here, Waddell hugs one of the four
figures of a group called "That which might
have been." He dedicated this inspirational
work to four little girls killed in the bombing
of a church in Alabama, in 1963. Another
casting of this group is to be installed in
front of the Civil Rights Center in
Birmingham, Ala.

(photo Michel F. Sarda)

Up from the deep old Earth I draw knowledge of things
Wonderful things I could never have known before.

Maynard Dixon

(above)
A special ordinance protects the towering landmark of Camelback Mountain.

(facing page)
Preserving the fragile natural environment has been an ongoing preoccupation for decades, a concern regularly challenged by a fast urban growth. In the 1970s, the Phoenix Mountain Preserve was created, transforming immense expanses of untouched wilderness into municipal parks, including the Squaw Peak range, in the heart of Greater Phoenix.

(photos Michel F. Sarda)

In all the earth no pulses beat
Except the trembling purple heat
Over the desert, and my own
Heart, quiet as a sunlit stone.

Harry Behn

The Desert Botanical Garden introduces its
visitors to the flora of the arid regions of the
Earth, and of the Sonoran desert. A renowned
research center, it is home to more than
20,000 plants representing 4,000 species.

(photo Michel F. Sarda)

70

The Phoenix Zoo was opened in 1962 and today is the largest, totally private zoo (no tax support) in the country.

Within a year of its founding, the Zoo was asked to become a sanctuary for nine of the last Arabian (white) oryx. It was estimated that there were no more than 50 of these animals left in the world. Since their arrival, this endangered species has thrived in the Arizona desert climate, and over 225 young animals have been raised in the Zoo's breeding program. In the 1970s, reintroductions back into the wild were successful. The Phoenix Zoo is proud to have been the "stationary ark" on which this wild and gracious animal was saved from extinction.

Warren J. Iliff
Executive Director, The Phoenix Zoo

Flamingos animate one of the various "theme" areas of The Phoenix Zoo.

(photo Michel F. Sarda)

LIVING THE QUALITY LIFE

Greater Phoenix is exactly what its residents want: a dynamic community that fosters success and guarantees a high quality of life. The effort required to create this environment has attracted considerable attention. The City of Phoenix was ranked as the Best Managed City in the U.S. and the World by the Bertelmann Foundation. Scottsdale was selected America's Most Livable City by the U.S. Council of Cities.

The region is energized by strong population growth, abundant recreational opportunities and comparatively new community resources. The prevailing positive attitude is irresistible, inviting involvement in every aspect of the community, from attending cultural events to volunteering at local charitable organizations.

Affordable housing is available at or below rates found in similar-sized regions. A seemingly endless variety of styles allows residents to select a house they truly can call "home." Master-planned communities are among the most popular housing locations; many include hiking and biking trails, golf courses, playgrounds, schools and other amenities designed for comfort and convenience.

More than 130 golf courses and upwards of 1,000 tennis courts allow residents to enjoy the ever sunny climate. Nearby deep-water lakes provide attractive settings for fishing, boating, swimming and water skiing. Sports "aficionados", also can opt to take life a little easier, serving as spectators for the region's professional basketball, football, hockey and baseball teams. Attendance at collegiate sporting events represents another popular entertainment option.

Perhaps the best attraction of all is available free of charge: a Greater Phoenix sunset. These evening spectaculars light up the sky with the vibrant colors of the Southwest.

(opposite page)
An Arizona sunset can be counted among the most magnificent sceneries Nature can offer. The fiery colors of this one evoke the legendary revival of the Phoenix bird from its ashes.
(photo Michel F. Sarda)

And then
All eyes turning toward the blazing sky
Of red and gold as the whole world
Filled with splendor,
All the universe could hold.

Hilda Faunce Wetherill

Then wise men turn and leave the noisy crowd,
And seek the quietude within God's templed groves,
The symphonies of peace upon the sea,
Or desert's hushed tranquility, and are sustained
To meet the ultimate of melody.

Vesta Hardy Vandeveer

Lifestyle

Something was different
Something had transpired
And we had been lucky
That we had been touched
By something
Richer and brighter
Than we had known before.

Robert Bear Miller

Beautiful nature, an ever-blue sky and a myriad of activities offer a unique lifestyle.
(preceding panel)
Pinnacle Peak, in north Scottsdale, offers a glorious natural environment to recent housing developments and to world-class golf courses.

(above, clockwise from top left)
Climbers of Phoenix and Tempe share Papago Mountain; participants in the annual WestWorld Arabian horse show; a sunbather enjoys one of the many man-made lakes surrounding Phoenix; children wonder at a bronze eagle at the Tempe Arts Festival.

(photos Michel F. Sarda)

(above)
Fox hunting in the Sonoran desert might be
the ultimate experience for horse riders.
(overleaf)
Bartlett Lake, 25 miles northeast of Phoenix,
is a favorite summer destination for boaters
and swimmers.

(photo Michel F. Sarda)

77

Blue are the hills of distance,
Distant and far away.
But close is home and hearthstone
Close as the close of day.
Milo Wiltbank

A delicate balance is necessary between the appealing desert and new residential developments, such as Troon Village, on the foothills of the McDowell Mountains.

(photo Michel F. Sarda)

Isn't there glory just in being
On a desert day like this?
Isn't this the quick of living,
Immediate bliss?

Margaret Erwin Schevill

The combination of the age-old adobe
construction technique with contemporary
forms creates stunningly inviting homes.

(photo Michel F. Sarda)

I want my house built high on a hill,
With an easy path to my door;
A path that youth and age can climb,
To sit with me in the evening time...
I want my house built high on a hill,
With the world spread out at my feet.

Charles S. Poling

(above)
Architects relish building homes in beautiful, challenging sites. Will Bruder, Antoine Predock have already contributed their talent to the design of outstanding residences throughout the Valley. The older Lykes House is vintage Frank Lloyd Wright.

(facing page)
Warm weather makes swimming pools an extension of the home most of the year.

(photo Michel F. Sarda)

Greater Phoenix is a shopper's heaven. The Valley offers several of the most successful shopping malls in the country, in a unique diversity of shops, styles and architecture.

(clockwise from top left)

The enclosed, air-conditioned mall of the Scottsdale Fashion Park; the Arizona Center is a successful addition to downtown Phoenix; the elegant Biltmore Fashion Park; the more casual, charming shops along Mill Avenue in Tempe.

(photos Michel F. Sarda)

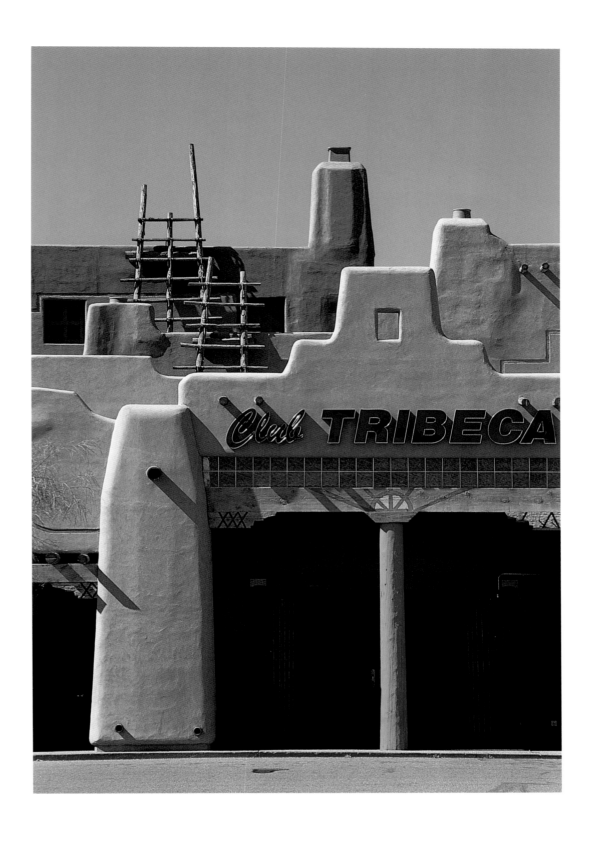

Papago Plaza in Scottsdale, by architect
DeRoy Mark, is a playful illustration of the
old territorial style.

(photo Michel F. Sarda)

When you've been coyotin' an' likkerin' up
An' the redeye's beginnin' to show,
When yore haid is aridin' plumb handsome an' high
But yore stummick is feelin' plumb low,
Jest swing into yore saddle an' haid for a bar.

Stan Adler

When it comes to dining, amateurs of the Old West are not disappointed: many restaurants and several theme parks offer the casual atmosphere of yesteryear.

(photo Michel F. Sarda)

(above)
Sophistication and culture are everywhere in
Greater Phoenix, and gastronomy is part of
it. Several restaurants rank among the best
in the country. Chefs Vincent Guérithault
and Christopher Gross have each earned a
national reputation with their own
restaurants. The Golden Swan, at the Hyatt
at Gainey Ranch in Scottsdale, offers a
romantic setting.

(overleaf)
Resorts like the Scottsdale Princess make
Greater Phoenix a destination of choice for
visitors from around the world.

(photo Michel F. Sarda)

87

The legendary San Marcos Resort was built by Dr. Alexander Chandler, founder of the city of Chandler, in the Mission Revival style. When it opened in 1913, it was the first Arizona resort to offer a full combination of amenities such as golf, tennis, horseback riding and polo games. In the late 1920s, Dr. Chandler invited Frank Lloyd Wright to design a new San Marcos. The project had to be cancelled because of financial difficulties related to the Great Depression.

Today, it is the Sheraton San Marcos Golf Resort and Conference Center.

(photo Michel F. Sarda)

Within this turquoise cup of day
No motion of the wind can sway
Or small sound quiver anywhere
The bright precision of the air.
Harry Behn

The Wigwam Resort in Litchfield Park is one
of the region's Five-Star resorts.
(photo Michel F. Sarda)

Several resorts offer spectacular water features, such as a waterfall at the Scottsdale Princess (left), or a sand beach pool at the Hyatt at Gainey Ranch (above).

(overleaf)

The Tradition Golf Tournament takes place every year on the two superb golf courses designed by Jack Nicklaus at Desert Mountain.

(photos Michel F. Sarda)

93

Because the desert is usually very dry and the ball travels higher and faster, you'll probably find that playing golf in the desert is easier. If not — well, just relax and enjoy the beautiful scenery.

Jack Nicklaus

(above)
The Barrett-Jackson Classic Car Auction
brings thousands of automobile fans to
WestWorld of Scottsdale every year.
(opposite page)
The Thunderbird Balloon Classic also takes
place at WestWorld.

(photo Michel F. Sarda)

96

Horses are daily companions for many Greater Phoenix residents. Areas are recognized as "horse property neighborhoods." Horse riding can be practiced nearly everywhere, in casual or sophisticated fashion. Here, a participant in the All-Arabian Horse Show waits for the decision of the jury.

(photo Michel F. Sarda)

A Bedouin legend has it that God grasped a handful of southerly wind, blew His breath across it and created the Arabian horse. Arabs call him the "Drinker of the Wind" for his endurance in the desert.

This radiant participant in the Fiesta Bowl Parade represents the numerous Arabian horse breeding farms that make Greater Phoenix one of the largest markets in the world for this valued animal.

(photo Ken Akers, courtesy of Fiesta Bowl)

Art is present in many public places and horses are a recurrent, extremely popular theme. "Bronco" by Phoenix artist Ed Mell, also well known for his majestic landscape paintings, was inspired by the crest of the City of Scottsdale.

(photo Michel F. Sarda)

100

*The things I know
are around me
like a blanket,
keeping me safe
from those things
which are strange.*
Ann Nolan Clark

With several art museums of national stature, more than a hundred art galleries, and several arts festivals and major shows each year, Greater Phoenix emerges as an important art market. Western and Cowboy Art lovers come from around the world to discover works such as *Rain-in-the-face*, a lifesize polychrome bronze by southwestern artist Dave McGary.

(photo Michel F. Sarda)

The tremendous energy inherent in these horses, which rise out of the earth, represents what we believe America and free enterprise are all about, and the deep connection between individual freedom and the indomitable spirit of the entrepreneur.

Morton H. Fleischer

These free horses exemplify the determination of the tightly-knit communities comprising Greater Phoenix in their unstoppable quest for a great future. *Spirit*, a life-size group of bronze horses by Arizona artist Buck McCain, graces the access to the Franchise Finance Corporation of America.

(photo Michel F. Sarda)

Business

Economic diversity provides Greater Phoenix with amazing market strength. The region's operating environment supports every imaginable type of business, from plastic extrusion to food processing, from fabricated metals to business services. Health care is also a notable growth industry.

Combined, these industries make this one of the most dynamic job markets in the United States. The broad economic base has allowed the area to develop one of the nation's most stable regional economies, a strong selling point to domestic and foreign investors alike.

Just a few of the corporations with local operations include: Motorola; Intel; Honeywell; McDonnell Douglas Helicopters; Karsten Manufacturing Corp., maker of Ping golf clubs; Revlon; General Motors; AT&T, and B.F. Goodrich. Renowned health-care facilities include the Mayo Clinic, Barrows Neurological Institute, the Menninger Clinic and the Arizona Heart Institute.

A growing population and healthy job creation, particularly in manufacturing, have made Greater Phoenix one of the nation's top retail markets. Power centers, regional malls and a host of smaller shopping centers provide instant consumer access to the latest product offerings. The comparatively low cost of doing business attracts new warehouse/distribution facilities every month.

Economic growth is being guided by the Governor's Strategic Partnership for Economic Development. This program has identified 10 business clusters in which Arizona has a competitive edge. Those clusters are: bioindustry, business services, environmental technology, food fiber and natural products, high-tech, minerals and mining, optics, tourism and experience, transportation and distribution and software.

Corporate buildings often are the most visible signature of a community's vitality.

(clockwise from top left)
Arizona Center; Bank One Center, the highest building in Arizona; reflections in the C.G. Rein Building in Scottsdale; Bank of America, the highest building in Mesa.

(facing page)
The twin towers of the Renaissance Center, downtown Phoenix, illustrate what John Nesbitt's *Megatrends 2000* heralded as one of the most promising metropolitan areas of the 21st century.

(photos Michel F. Sarda)

POSITIONED FOR SUCCESS

Greater Phoenix couldn't be in a better position. Simple geography makes it a strategic choice to access major commercial and travel centers. Developed air and ground transportation systems support a fast-growing trading hub, allowing companies to efficiently reach destinations throughout the world.

Those destinations include southern California, the southwestern Sun Belt, Mexico, Canada, Europe and the Pacific Rim. Los Angeles is an hour away by air. Western U.S. states adjoining Arizona form a consumer market of more than 41 million people. Greater Phoenix is a major stop along the 2,000-mile Canamex Corridor, a fact made all the more significant with the passage of the North American Free Trade Agreement. Several hundred common and custom carriers, as well as two transcontinental railways, are available to deliver goods to key West Coast ports for export to foreign countries. Freight also is shipped through Phoenix Sky Harbor International Airport, one of the nation's busiest airports — in both cargo and passengers. This facility is the headquarters for America West Airlines and the largest hub in Southwest Airlines' operation. Competition between these air carriers and others keep fares comparatively low. A third runway is further increasing the airport's efficiency.

Six interstate highways cross the state, making Greater Phoenix a haven for all types of distribution activities. Warehouses stocked with everything from toys to soft drinks prove the ability of the region to deliver the world to its resident corporations.

Sky Harbor International Airport serves Greater Phoenix, and is one of the busiest in the world. It is home to America West Airlines.
(photo Michel F. Sarda)

106

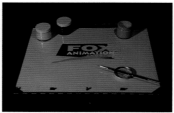

Represented here by their logos, these corporations are among those calling Greater Phoenix home.

(photos Michel F. Sarda)

We of humankind
hearts quickened to compassion
hope with inward vision kindled
to risk
the searching of our souls
to dare
the unexpected
to master
barb and thorn
and hear the whisper of eternity.

Trevor Southey
(carved in the base of the sculpture in front of Renaissance Center)

A sophisticated corporate environment, such as The Renaissance Center, downtown Phoenix, complements the casual and friendly southwestern way of doing business.

(photo Michel F. Sarda)

109

Major corporations contribute to the local economy.

(photos Michel F. Sarda)

The health care revolution is alive and well in Greater Phoenix. Economic growth, expanding employers seeking cost-effective health benefits, and extensive managed care experience make this a center for health care innovation and development. By 1992, Arizona was ranked as the nation's 8th-largest market for private managed care networks. The state's innovative Medicaid program — the Arizona Health Care Cost Containment Program — based on a capitated payment model with services furnished by private provider networks, furthered the managed care trend.

Health care providers have been innovative in developing the provider networks and information systems necessary to manage care. Almost 15 years' participation with AHCCCS has given hospitals and physicians extensive experience in delivering care to patients across the health care spectrum, while keeping costs down. As the Valley continues to grow, health care service delivery will continue to evolve to meet those needs — and it is a good bet that the area will remain in the forefront of groundbreaking health care networks and financing.

Beth Schermer
Lewis and Roca LLP

(above)
Mayo Clinic Scottsdale is one among many state-of-the-art medical facilities that have made Greater Phoenix a major medical center.
(overleaf)
The sun plays visual games in the glass walls of the Esplanade buildings, a corporate center designed by Cornoyer Hedrick Architects.

(photo Michel F. Sarda)

Appendices

Translations
French
Spanish
German
Japanese
Chinese

General Index of Names

Note of the Publisher

It is our hope that these illustrated translations will contribute to the satisfaction of international readers. In regard to the available space, it was not possible to accommodate the translation of all the texts, tributes and quotations appearing throughout this book.

Translations

French
Spanish
German
Japanese
Chinese

Chinese translation
sponsored by
Continental Circuits Corp.

pages 18-19

Camelback Mountain était un site sacré pour les anciens habitants de la Vallée.

Camelback Mountain era un lugar sagrado para los habitantes antiguos.

Camelback Mountain war ein geheiligter Ort für Bewohner aus früherer Zeit.

古代のインディアンにとって聖地であったキャメルバック・マウンテン。

駱駝山 (Cambelback Mountain) 對先民而言是一處聖地。

page 20

Tous les printemps, une délicate floraison embellit et colore les cactus.

Cada primavera, delicadas flores adornan la chumbera.

Jedes Frühjahr blühen zarte Blüten auf dem "prickly pear" Kaktus.

毎年、春を迎え、可憐な花を咲かせるプリックリーペア・サボテン。

每年春天，〝刺梨〞仙人掌嬌嫩的花便綻開。

page 21

Les traditions indiennes sont présentes dans beaucoup d'aspects de la vie quotidienne en Arizona.

Culturas indígenas americanas influyen en muchos aspectos de la vida en Arizona.

Die Kulturen der ersten indianischen Bewohner durchdringen viele Aspekte des Lebens in Arizona.

ネイティブ・アメリカンの文化がアリゾナでの生活に様々な影響を与える。

印第安人文化溶入到許多亞利桑那州的生活層面。

page 22

Le jésuite Eusebio Kino reste une figure lumineuse de l'Arizona d'autrefois.

El jesuita Eusebio Kino es una figura brillante en la historia temprana de Arizona.

Der Jesuit Eusebio Kino ist eine strahlende Figur des frühen Arizona.

イエズス会のエウセビオ・キノ神父は初期のアリゾナ史において光彩を放つ人物である。

捷蘇以色比歐基諾 (Jesult Eusebio Kino) 是亞利桑那州早期的一位著名人物。

page 23

L'eau et le cheval ont joué un rôle essentiel dans l'établissement des pionniers.

Caballos y agua eran factores principales en atraer a los pobladores a esta tierra.

Pferde und Wasser spielten eine entscheidende Rolle Siedler für Arizona zu gewinnen.

馬と水がこの土地に開拓者達を魅了するための重要な役割を果たしている。

馬和水在吸引移民者到此地來扮演了一個重要的角色。

page 24

Les deux tours de la Basilique Sainte-Marie appartiennent au paysage du centre de Phoenix.

Las dos torres de la Basílica de Santa María son un monumento popular del centro de Phoenix.

Die beiden Türme der St Mary's Basilika sind ein bekanntes Wahrzeichen in downtown Phoenix.

セント・メリー・バスティリカの二つの塔はフェニックスのダウンタウンのポピュラーな見所となっている。

聖馬利貝斯里卡 (St. Mary's Basilica)的兩座塔是鳳凰城市中心一處有名的市標。

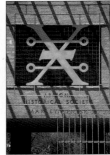

page 25

Le Capitole fut construit après que Phoenix fût devenu la capitale du territoire d'Arizona en 1890. Le statut d'Etat ne fut obtenu qu'en 1912.

El edificio del Capitolio fue construido después que Phoenix se erigiera en capital territorial de Arizona en 1890. En 1912, Arizona se proclamó estado.

Das Kapitol wurde im Jahr 1890 erbaut, nachdem Phoenix die Hauptstadt des Territoriums Arizona geworden war. Als Staat wurde Arizona im Jahr 1912 aufgenommen.

州庁舎はフェニックスが1890年にアリゾナ準州の州都に制定された後に建設された。

州政府大樓 (Capitol building) 是在1890年鳳凰城成爲亞利桑那州的首府後建造的，1912年則正式成立爲一州。

pages 26-27

La maison de l'artiste Jessie Benton Evans devint en 1927 un élégant hôtel. L'Auberge de Jokake constitue aujourd'hui une curiosité sur la propriété de l'Hotel Phoenicien.

La casa del artista Jessie Benton Evans pasó a ser un hotel elegante en 1927. Jokake Inn es ahora en los jardines del Phoenician Resort.

Das Haus des Künstlers Jessie Benton Evans wurde im Jahr 1927 ein elegantes Ferienhotel. Das Jokake Inn ist heute ein reizvolles Wahrzeichen auf dem Gelände des Phoenician Resort.

芸術家ジェシー・ベントン・エバンスの家は1927年にエレガントなリゾートとなる。ジョカケ・インが今ではフェニッシアン・リゾートの敷地内で興味ある建物となっている。

喬科克旅館 (Jokake Inn) 是藝術家杰西班頓依芳 (Jessie Benton Evans) 的家。在1927年，它成爲一處雅緻的勝地。現今在鳳凰城的度假勝地中這座古老的土磚建築物是一處迷人的旅遊景點。

page 28

Le Musée de la Société d'Histoire de l'Arizona, dans Papago Park, présente au visiteur divers aspects de l'histoire locale.

El museo de la Sociedad Histórica de Arizona en el parque Pápago presenta al visitante varios aspectos de la historia de Arizona.

Das Museum der Arizona Historical Society im Papago Park stellt dem Besucher verschiedene Aspekte des Lebens in Arizona vor.

パパゴ・パークにあるアリゾナ歴史協会博物館ではビジターにアリゾナの歴史を紹介している。

在帕帕格公園 (Papago Park) 的亞利桑那社會歷史博物館向參觀者展示了亞利桑那歷史的多重風貌。

page 29

Le Musée Heard a été initialement fondé en 1929 pour abriter la collection d'objets indiens rassemblée par Dwight et Maie Heard.

El Museo Heard fue inicialmente fundado en 1929 para albergar la colección de los artefactos americanos de Dwight y Maie Heard.

Das Heard Museum wurde im Jahr 1929 gegründet, um die Sammlung von Gegenständen aus dem Leben früher indianischer Bewohner zu beherbergen.

ハード博物館は最初インディアンに関連する展示物を公開するために1929年にハード夫妻宅に設立された。

哈特博物館 (Heard Museum) 是在1929年 爲杜懷特 (Dwight) 和梅爾哈特 (Male Heard) 收藏的美國工藝品而設立的。

page 30

Achevé en 1929 avec l'assistance de l'architecte Frank Lloyd Wright, l'hôtel Arizona Biltmore est encore l'un des plus prestigieux d'Amérique.

Terminado en 1929, con la ayuda del architecto Frank Lloyd Wright, el Arizona Biltmore es uno de los hoteles más prestigiosos del país.

Das Arizona Biltmore ist heute eines der angesehensten Ferienhotels des Landes, es wurde vollendet im Jahr 1929 unter der Mitarbeit von Frank Lloyd Wright.

アリゾナ・ビルトモア・ホテルはフランク・ロイド・ライトのサポートを受け、1929年に完成し、全米でも最も格式のあるリゾートとなった。

1929年在法蘭克洛依德建造商 (Frank Lloyd Wright) 的協助下，亞利桑那巴爾的摩 (Biltmore) 成爲國內頗負勝名的觀光飯店。

page 31

Frank Lloyd Wright a fait de Taliesin West son séjour hivernal à partir de 1937.

Frank Lloyd Wright estableció Taliesin West como su base invernal en 1937.

Frank Lloyd Wright errichtete Taliesin West als seinen Wintersitz im Jahr 1937.

フランク・ロイド・ライトは1937年にタリアッセン・ウエストを避寒用の家として建築した。

1937年法蘭克洛依德建造商 (Frank Lloyd Wright) 建立塔黎鄂森維斯特 (Taliesin West) 以作爲他的避寒勝地。

page 32

Les étudiants indiens sont honorés par les représentants de leurs nations lors du rassemblement annuel à l'Université de l'Etat d'Arizona.

Los indigenas americanos reciben reconocimiento de sus pares en la asamblea ceremonial annual en la Universidad Estatal de Arizona.

Die Ureinwohner Amerikas, die Indianer, erhalten Zuspruch von ihren Mitbürgern beim jährlichen pow-wow an der Arizona State University.

ネイティブ・アメリカンがアリゾナ州立大学で開催される恒例のパウワウで仲間から祝福を受けている。

印第安人在亞利桑那州立大學的印第安人年會中得到的表揚。

page 33

Les rodéos perpétuent l'esprit du Far-West.

Los rodeos perpetuán el espíritu del Viejo Oeste.

Rodeos lassen den Geist des alten Westens weiterleben.

ロデオは古き西部のスピリットを継承している。

馴馬術的傳統使古老西部的精神流傳不朽。

page 34

Le désert environnant ressemble davantage à un jardin qu'à une étendue sauvage et hostile.

El desierto circundante parece más un jardín que un páramo hostil.

Die umgebende Wüste sieht mehr wie ein Garten als wie eine feindliche Wildnis aus.

砂漠は荒涼とした野性の景色というよりも、むしろガーデンといったほうが正しいかもしれない。

環繞周圍的沙漠看來更像一座花園而非一片荒地。

page 35

Le nouvel Hotel de Ville de Phoenix voisine élégamment avec le Théatre de l'Orpheon entièrement restauré.

El nuevo Ayuntamiento de Phoenix armoniza bien con el renovado Teatro Orpheon.

Das neue Rathaus von Phoenix verbindet sich harmonisch mit dem neu renovierten Orpheon Theater.

新しいフェニックス市庁舎が改築されたオープコン劇場の背景とやさしくマッチしている。

新的市府大樓柔和地與整修後的歐菲恩(Orpheon)劇院融合一體。

page 36

La perspective de Central Avenue et du centre de Phoenix témoigne d'une intense vitalité urbaine.

La perspectiva de la Avenida Central y la vista de los edificios del centro de Phoenix mustran vitalidad urbana.

Die Ansicht von Central Avenue und die Skyline von downtown Phoenix zeigt städtisches Leben.

セントラル．アベニューの眺望とフェニックスのダウンタウンの高層ビル群が都会のバイタリティーを象徴している。

中央林蔭大道和鳳凰城市中心的天景輪廓呈現著都市的生命力。

page 38

Les "sauteurs de flaques" de l'artiste Glenna Goodacre apportent une joyeuse animation dans les jardins du siège de Dial Corp.

Los "saltadores de charco" de la artista Glenna Goodacre dan vida a los terrenos de la oficina central de Dial Corp.

Die "Puddle Jumpers" (Pfützenspringer) der Künstlerin Glenna Goodacre bringen Leben auf den Gelände der Hauptverwaltung der Dial Corp.

芸術家のグレナ・グーダクレ作による"パドル・ジャンパー"がダイアル・コーポレーションの本社ビルに活気をもたらしている。

藝術家葛蘭娜(Glenna Goodacre)創作的 "Puddle Jumpers" 為黛爾(Dial Corp) 總部所在地增添了生氣。

page 39

Patriot Square au centre de Phoenix est un endroit populaire pour toutes sortes d'activités.

La Plaza Patriot, en el centro de Phoenix, es un lugar preferido para una variedad de eventos populares.

Patriot Square in downtown Phoenix ist einer der Orte, die für eine Vielzahl von beliebte Veranstaltungen zur Verfügung stehen.

フェニックスのダウンタウンにあるパトリオット・スクエアーでは種々のポピュラーなイベントが開催される。

鳳凰城市中心的愛國廣場(Patriot Square) 是眾多活動的聚點。

page 40

La population du Grand Phoenix est une des plus jeunes parmi les grandes agglomérations des Etats-Unis.

La población de Phoenix metropolitano está entre las más jóvenes de los Estados Unidos.

Die Bevölkerung von Gesamt-Phoenix gehört zu den jüngsten der ganzen Vereinigten Staaten.

フェニックス大都市圏に住む市民は全米でも最も若い。

大鳳凰城的人口在美國算是最年輕的。

page 41

L'équipe de basket-ball des Phoenix Suns bénéficie d'un évident soutien local.

Los Phoenix Suns reciben un fuerte apoyo de la communidad.

Die Phoenix Suns werden von der Bevölkerung kräftig unterstützt.

フェニックス・サンズは地元で強力な支持を受けている。

鳳凰城太陽籃球代表隊受到社區廣大的 支持。

page 42

Dans les années 20, des indiens Yaqui, réfugiés du Mexique, fondèrent la pittoresque petite communauté de Guadalupe, au sud de Tempe.

En los principios de los años 20, los refugiados yaqui establicieron un pintoresco barrio de Guadalupe, al sur de Tempe.

In den frühen 20iger Jahren gründeten Yaqui-Flüchtlinge die farbenfrohe Gemeinde Guadalupe, südlich von Tempe.

1920年代初頭、ヤキ・インディアンの非難民達はテンピ市の南に位置するグアダルペにカラフルなコミュニティーを築き上げた。

1920年代早期雅各(Yaqui)的難民在天庇城(Tempe)南方的夸達魯貝 (Guadalupe)建立了多采多姿的社區。

page 43

Chaque année, le festival de l'Etoile du Matin est une occasion pour les Indiens d'Amérique de se retrouver et de célébrer leurs traditions.

Cada año, el festival de Morning Star es una ocasión para los indígenas americanos a reunirse y celebrar sus tradiciones.

Jedes Jahr ist das Fest des "Morning Star" (Morgenstern) eine Gelegenheit für Indianer sich zu treffen und ihre Bräuche zu feiern.

毎年モーニング・スター・フェスティバルはネイティブ・アメリカンが集い伝統を祝うための行事となっている。

每年晨星節是印第安人齊聚一堂並慶祝其傳統的時刻。

page 44

La qualité remarquable des espaces urbains du centre de Phoenix a reçu une reconnaissance nationale.

La excelente cualidad de los espacios urbanos del centro de Phoenix recibió reconocimiento nacional.

Die hervorragende Qualität von städtischen Plätzen in downtown Phoenix erhielt nationale Anerkennung.

フェニックスのダウンタウンの質の高い都市開発は全米で高い評価を受けている。

鳳凰城市中心高品質的都市空間全國有口皆碑。

page 45

Les jardins de l'Arizona Center sont une oasis de calme et de fraîcheur.

Los jardines de Arizona Center ofrecen espacios frescos y tranquilos.

Die Gärten des Arizona Center sorgen für Ruhe und Kühle.

アリゾナ・センターの中庭は清涼さと静寂さをかもし出している。

亞利桑那中心(Arizona Center)的花園提供了一處涼爽、怡靜的空間。

page 46

Les lapins géants de l'artiste Mark Rossi ont été immédiatement acceptés dans le paysage urbain de Tempe.

Las liebres de bronce, de tamaño mayor que el natural, del artista Mark Rossi, se convirtieron instantáneamente en un monumento en Tempe.

Die überlebensgrossen Jackrabbits aus Bronze von dem Künstler Mark Rossi wurden augenblicklich zu einem Wahrzeichen in Tempe.

芸術家マーク・ロッシ作による実物より大きなブロンズのジャックラビットがテンピ市の興味深い見世物となっている。

藝術家馬克羅西(Mark Rossi)雕塑的一座比實物還大的野兔銅像立即成為天庇城(Tempe)的城標。

page 47

"Dimanche sur Central Avenue" attire des résidents de tous les quartiers.

El "Domingo en la Avenida Central" atrae a los residentes de todo el Valle.

"Sonntag auf Central Avenue" lockt Bewohner aus dem ganzen Tal an.

"サンデー・オン・セントラル・アベニュー"が街中から市民を魅了している。

"星期天的中央大道"吸引了廣大的當地居民。

page 48

Les villes qui composent le Grand Phoenix montrent une grande vitalité pour construire des équipements à la fois beaux et attractifs.

Las comunidades que forman parte de Phoenix metropolitano muestran gran vitalidad en construir espacios y amenidades atractivas.

Gemeinden, die zusammen Gesamt-Phoenix bilden zeigen große Lebensfreude beim Bau einladender Plätze und Einrichtungen für die Bewohner.

フェニックス大都市圏を包含するコミュニティーの建築ラッシュが力強いバイタリティーを見せている。

包括大鳳凰城的社區從寬敞舒適的建築物中展示著生機活力。

page 49

L'importante population estudiantine de Tempe a adopté Hayden Square pour se rassembler et s'amuser.

La gran población estudiantil en Tempe ha elegido la Plaza Hayden como lugar de diversión y entretenimiento.

Die zahlreiche Studentenschaft Tempes hat sich den Hayden Square als Treffpunkt für Spaß und Unterhaltung ausgesucht.

テンピ市の巨大な学生人口のためにヘイデン・スクエアが建築され学生達の憩と遊びの場となっている。

天庇城的眾多學生選擇海敦廣場(Hayden Square)作為他們閑暇時的娛樂場所。

pages 50-51

L'équipe des Phoenix Suns est ici opposée aux Houston Rockets dans l'America West Arena.

Los Phoenix Suns luchan contra los Houston Rockets en el estadio de America West.

Die Phoenix Suns im Wettkampf mit den Houston Rockets in der America West Arena.

アメリカ・ウエスト・アリーナではフェニックス・サンズがヒューストン・ロケッツと試合をしている。

鳳凰城太陽隊(Phoenix Suns)與休士頓洛克(Houston Rockets)在美西廣場(America West Arena)交鋒。

page 52

La Ligue du Cactus fait venir plusieurs grandes équipes de baseball pour leur entraînement de printemps.

La Liga Cactus trae al Valle varios equipos principales de béisbol para el entrenamiento primaveral.

Die Cactus League bringt mehrere Major League Baseball Mannschaften in das Tal zum Frühjahrstraining.

キャクタス・リーグが春季トレーニングのために幾つかの大リーグチームをバレー・オブ・ザ・サンと呼ばれるこの地に招いている。

仙人掌隊(Cactus League) 每年邀請數支主要棒球隊到山谷來進行春季集訓。

page 53

Des équipements sportifs ultra-modernes existent dans la plupart des villes du Grand Phoenix.

Las modernísimas facilidades deportivas se pueden encontrar en la mayoría de las poblaciones del Valle del Sol.

Sportanlagen auf dem neusten Stand kann man in den meisten Städten des "Valley of the Sun" (Tal der Sonne) finden.

最新鋭のスポーツ施設がフェニックス大都市圏のいたる所で見られる。

在太陽谷地區的絕大城鎮都有各種現代化的運動設施。

page 54

Au début de chaque année, les célébrations du Fiesta Bowl attirent des dizaines de milliers de résidents et de visiteurs.

Al terminar cada año, los eventos de Fiesta Bowl atraen miles de residentes y visitantes.

Bei jedem Jahreswechsel ist die Fiesta Bowl und ihre Veranstaltungen eine Attraktion für Tausende von Bewohnern und Besuchern.

毎年年末に開催されるフィエスタボールが何千人もの市民と観光客を魅了している。

一年一度的費思塔盃(Fiesta Bowl)活動，吸引著數以千計的居民和遊客。

page 55

Le Sun Devil Stadium, le stade aux 75.000 places de l'Université de l'état d'Arizona, a été sélectionné pour le Super Bowl 1996.

El estadio de Sun Devils de la Universidad Estatal de Arizona, con capacidad de 75.000, fue elegido para el partido de NFL Super Bowl de 1996.

Das Sun Devil Stadion, das 75.000 Plätze enthält, wurde für das Super Bowl Spiel im Jahr 1996 ausgewählt.

アリゾナ州立大学の七万五千席を有するサンデビル・スタジアムが1996年度のNFLスーパーボールの開催地として選出された。

亞利桑那州立大學可容納七萬五千個座位的魔神太陽(Sun Devil)露天運動場被選爲1996年職業橄欖球超級盃決賽地點。

page 56

La nouvelle bibliothèque municipale de Phoenix a fait les gros titres des magazines d'architecture pour la qualité de sa conception.

La nueva Biblioteca Central de Phoenix apareció en primera plana de las revistas de arquitectura.

Das neue Gebäude der Stadtbücherei von Phoenix machte Schlagzeilen in Architekturzeitschriften.

新しくなったフェニックス・セントラル図書館は建築関係の雑誌で脚光を浴びている。

新的鳳凰城中央圖書館登上建築雜誌的頭條新聞。

page 57

L'école "Thunderbird" de gestion internationale offre aussi une variété de services aux sociétés américaines.

"Thunderbird" (American Graduate School of International Management) presta un valioso servicio a las empresas de negocio americanas.

"Thunderbird", die American Graduate School for International Management ist eine wichtige Bezugsquelle für amerikanische Firmen.

アメリカ経営大学院("サンダーバード校")は米国ビジネスの重要な資源である。

美國國際管理研究院 -- 雷鳥研究院 (American Graduate School of International Management-Thunderbird）爲美國商界主要資訊來源。

page 58

Le Grand Phoenix offre un choix remarquable d'établissements scolaires et universitaires de haut niveau.

Phoenix metropolitano ofrece una excelente selección de facilidades educativas.

Gesamt-Phoenix bietet eine ausgezeichnete Auswahl an Ausbildungsstätten.

フェニックス大都市圏では様々な傑出した教育施設を提供している。

大鳳凰城給教育界提供了一個優越的選擇。

page 59

L'auditorium Grady Gammage, sur le campus de l'Université de l'état d'Arizona, a été conçu par Frank Lloyd Wright.

El auditorio de Grady Gammage Memorial, diseñado por Frank Lloyd Wright.

Das Grady Gammage Auditorium, das von Frank Lloyd Wright entworfen wurde.

グラディー・ガメッジ記念講堂はフランク・ロイド・ライトによる設計である。

葛瑞迪蓋米菊紀念館(Grady Gammage）是由法蘭克洛依德 (Frank Lloyd Wright) 設計的。

page 61

A partir de leur importante collection personnelle, Donna and Morton Fleischer ont créé un musée consacré aux peintres impressionnistes de Californie.

Los coleccionistas de arte Donna y Morton Fleischer han aportado un nuevo museo dedicado al impresionismo californiano.

Die Kunstsammler Donna und Morton Fleischer haben ein neues Museum gestiftet, das kalifornischen Impressionisten gewidmet ist.

芸術作品の収集家であるドナおよびモートン・フレイシャーは新しい美術館をカリフォルニアの印象主義派の画家達のために寄贈した。

藝術收藏家唐拿(Donna)和摩頓(Morton Fleischer) 為加州印象派畫家捐贈了一所新博物館。

page 62

Les arts et la communauté des artistes ont une part importante dans l'identité du Grand Phoenix.

Las artes y los artistas tienen un rol central en la comunidad de Phoenix metropolitano.

Die Kunst und Künstler spielen eine zentrale Rolle in dem Gemeindeleben von Gesamt-Phoenix.

芸術と芸術家がフェニックス大都市圏のコミュニティーで中心的な役割を果たしている。

藝術品和藝術家在大鳳凰城區扮演了一個中心角色。

page 63

Une scène de l'extraordinaire *Dracula* produit par l'Arizona Theatre Company (ATC).

Una escena de la extraordinaria producción de Drácula por la Compañia de Teatro de Arizona.

Eine Szene der hervorragenden Inszenierung von "Dracula" der Arizona Theatre Company.

アリゾナ・シアター・カンパニーによるドラキュラの優れた制作シーン。

由亞利桑那戲劇公司製作的吸血鬼 (Dracula)非凡的一幕作品。

page 64

L'artiste Fritz Scholder dans son studio de Scottsdale.

El artista Fritz Scholder en su estudio de Scottsdale.

Der Künstler Fritz Scholder in seinem Atelier in Scottsdale.

芸術家フリッツ・ショルダー、スコッツデールのアトリエにて。

藝術家佛瑞茲史高德(Fritz Scholder) 在斯卡茨得爾 (Scottsdale) 設有畫室。

page 65

L'architecte visionnaire Paolo Soleri accueille de jeunes visiteurs de sa Fondation Cosanti à Scottsdale.

El visionario arquitecto Paolo Soleri da la bienvenida a los jóvenes visitantes de su Fundación Cosanti de Scottsdale.

Der visionäre Architekt Paolo Soleri heißt junge Besucher auf dem Gelände seiner Cosanti Stiftung in Scottsdale willkommen.

視覚的建築家であるパオロ・ソレリが創設したコサンティ・ファウンデーションの敷地で若い訪問者を歓迎している。

幻覺建築師派奧羅塞樂利 (Paolo Soleri) 在他斯卡茨得爾科桑迩(Scottsdale Cosanti)基金會歡迎年輕參訪者。

page 66

Philip Curtis a été parmi les premiers grands artistes à s'établir en Arizona.

Philip C. Curtis fue entre los primeros grandes artistas que se establecieron en Arizona.

Philip C. Curtis war unter den ersten bekannten Künstlern, die sich in Arizona angesiedelt haben.

フィリップ・C・カーティス氏はアリゾナに最も初期に移住した最初の著名な芸術家である。

飛利浦(Philip C. Curtis) 是最早移居 亞利桑那的主要藝術家之一 。

page 67

Les bronzes de John Waddell se reconnaissent dans de nombreuses résidences et lieux publics du Grand Phoenix.

Las figuras de John Waddell pueden verse en muchas casas y lugares públicos de Phoenix metropolitano.

John Waddells Figuren kann man in vielen Häusern und öffentlichen Plätzen in Phoenix sehen.

ジョン・ワデル氏の姿はフェニックス大都市圏内の数多くの住宅および公共の場所で見ることができる。

約翰華德(John Waddell) 的作品可以在大鳳凰城許多住家和公共場合看到。

page 68

Une ordonnance municipale protège la silhouette imposante et reconnaissable de Camelback Mountain.

Una ordenanza especial protege la imponente mole de Camelback Mountain.

Eine besondere Verordnung schützt den hoch aufragenden Camelback Mountain.

そびえ立つミャメルバック・マウンテンが特別条例により保護されいる。

法令特別名文規定保護高聳的駱駝山(Camelback Mountain) 。

page 69

Dans les années 70, la Phoenix Mountain Preserve a été créée pour transformer de vastes étendues de désert en parcs municipaux.

En los años 70, se creó el coto de la zonas montañosas de Phoenix, transformando immensos terrenos del desierto en parques municipales.

In den 70iger Jahren wurde das Phoenix Mountain Naturschutzgebiet geschaffen, das riesige Weiten von unberührter Wildnis in kommunale Naturschutzparks verwandelte.

1970年代にフェニックス・マウンテンリザーブが創設され、未踏の原野が市営公園と変化した。

1970年代首創鳳凰城山地保護機構，以巨額費用將純荒地改良成公園。

page 70

Le Jardin Botanique du Désert présente aux visiteurs la flore du désert de Sonora.

Desert Botanical Garden presenta a sus visitantes la vegetación del desierto de Sonora.

Der Desert Botanical Garden macht Besucher mit der Flora der Sonora Wüste bekannt.

デザート・ボタニカル・ガーデン(砂漠博物館)ではそこを訪れる人々にソノラン砂漠の植物を紹介している。

波頓尼可沙漠(Desert Botanical)花園向遊覽者介紹在瑟柔蘭(Sonoran)沙漠裡的花卉。

page 71

Des flamands roses animent l'un des secteurs "à thème" du zoo de Phoenix.

Flamencos animan una de las varias partes del parque temático del Zoológico de Phoenix.

Flamingos beleben eine der zahlreichen nach Themen ange-ordneten Bereiche des Phoenix Zoos.

フラミンゴがフェニックス動物園にある様々な"テーマ"地区を活気づけている。

紅鶴是亞利桑那動物園多種"主題區"中的明星。

page 73

Un coucher de soleil d'Arizona compte probablement parmi ce que la nature peut offrir de plus spectaculaire.

Una puesta de sol en Arizona esta una de las más impresionantes vistas que la naturaleza puede ofrecer.

Zu den herrlichsten Szenen, die die Natur bieten kann, kann man einen Sonnenuntergang in Arizona zählen.

アリゾナの夕日は自然が織り成す最も雄大な景観であるといえる。

亞利桑那的夕陽堪稱自然界最壯麗的景觀之一。

pages 74-75

Pinnacle Peak, dans le nord de Scottsdale, offre un environnement naturel unique pour de nouveaux quartiers résidentiels et des parcours de golf de classe internationale.

Pinnacle Peak, en el norte de Scottsdale, ofrece un glorioso medio ambiente natural para la reciente urbanización y para los clubs de golf de categoría mundial.

Pinnacle Peak in Nord-Scottsdale bietet eine herrliche Umgebung für unlängst gebaute Wohngegenden und Weltklasse-Golfplätze.

スコッツデールの北にあるピナクルピークが近年の住宅開発と世界的なレベルのゴルフコースに雄大な自然環境を提供している。

比那口山峰(Pinnacle Peak),位在北斯卡茨得爾(North Scottsdale),提供一個優雅自然的居住環境和世界級的網球場。

page 76

Une nature superbe, un ciel toujours bleu et une myriade de choses à faire font bénéficier les résidents du Grand Phoenix d'un mode de vie unique.

Una naturaleza preciosa, un cielo azul siempre presente y una variedad de actividades brindan un estilo de vida inigualable.

Bewundernswerte Natur, ein ewig blauer Himmel und eine Vielzahl von Aktivitäten bieten einen einzigartigen Lebenstil.

美しい自然、澄みきった青空、豊富なアクティビティーによりユニークなライフスタイルが享受できる。

美麗的大自然，湛藍的天空，和無數的活動，提供一種獨特的生活型態。

page 77

Chasser à courre dans le désert de Sonora pourrait bien être le rêve ultime d'un cavalier.

La caceria de zorros en el desierto de Sonora podría ser la experiencia máxima para los jinetes.

Fuchsjagd in der Sonora-Wüste mag das höchste Erlebnis für Reiter sein.

ソノラン砂漠で行うキツネ狩りは乗馬をする人にとっては最高の経験であるといえる。

在瑟柔蘭沙漠(Sonoran desert)打獵也許是騎馬者最美好的經驗。

pages 78-79

En été, le lac Bartlett attire un grand nombre de nageurs et plaisanciers.

El lago Bartlett es la destinación favorita de verano para los aficionados a la náutica y a la natación.

Der Bartlett See ist ein bevorzugtes Sommerziel für Bootfahrer und Schwimmer.

バートレット湖はボート乗りや水泳をする人達にとってはお気に入りの場所である。

巴特列湖(Bartlett Lake)是夏季最受喜愛游泳和游湖人士歡迎的地方。

page 80

Un équilibre délicat doit être observé entre l'écologie du désert et la création de nouveaux quartiers résidentiels.

Es necesario un equilibrio delicado entre un atrayente desierto y las nuevas urbanizaciones residenciales.

Ein empfindliches Gleichgewicht muss zwischen der reizvollen Wüste und den neu erstandenen Wohngebieten bestehen.

砂漠と新しい開発地域の間ではデリケートなバランスが必要とされる。

在令人喜愛的沙漠和新社區發展之間適宜的平衡是必要的。

page 81

L'ancienne technique de construction d'adobe permet toujours de réaliser des résidences d'une extraordinaire beauté.

La antiquísima técnica de construcción de adobe produce casas de una belleza deslumbrante.

Die uralte Adobebautechnik schafft verblüffend schöne Häuser.

古き時代のアドビ建築技術が素晴しい美を創造している。

古老的磚造技術造就了美麗的住房。

page 82

Lykes House est signée du meilleur Frank Lloyd Wright.

Lykes House constituye lo clásico de Frank Lloyd Wright.

Lykes Haus ist ein früher Frank Lloyd Wright.

ライクス・ハウスはフランク・ロイド・ライトの傑作である。

萊克斯房屋 (Lykes House)是的法蘭克洛依德(Frank Lloyd Wright)的醇建地。

page 83

La clémence du climat fait de la piscine un prolongement de la maison.

El clima caliente convierte las piscinas en una extensión de la casa.

Das warme Wetter macht die Schwimmbäder zu einem weiteren Wohnraum.

温暖な気候のためプールが家の一部となっている。

溫暖的氣候使得游泳池變成家庭的一部分。

page 84

Le Grand Phoenix est un paradis pour les amateurs de shopping.

Phoenix metropolitano es un paraíso del comprador.

Gesamt-Phoenix ist ein Paradies zum Einkaufen.

フェニックス大都市圏はショッピングをする人にとってはパラダイスである。

大鳳凰城 (Greater Phoenix)是購物者的天堂。

page 85

Papago Plaza à Scottsdale reproduit avec humour le vieux style territorial.

Plaza Pápago en Scottsdale es una ilustración divertida del viejo estilo territorial.

Der Papago Plaza in Scottsdale ist ein verspieltes Beispiel des Stils des alten Territoriums.

スコッツデールにあるパパゴ・プラザでは古き準州時代の良さがしのばれる。

座落在斯卡茨得爾(Scottsdale)的帕帕格宮殿 (Papago Plaza)是舊式地方風格的展現。

page 86

De nombreux restaurants et parcs d'attractions font revivre l'atmosphère particulière du Far West.

Muchos restaurantes y parques temáticos hacen revivir el ambiente informal del Viejo Oeste.

Viele Restaurants und Parks lassen die lässige Atmosphäre des alten Westens wiederaufleben.

多くのレストランとテーマ・パークが古き西部のカジュアルな雰囲気の中で蘇っている。

許多餐廳和主題公園重現老西部的輕鬆氣氛。

page 87

Le restaurant du Cygne d'Or, au Hyatt de Scottsdale, offre un cadre parfait pour le plus romantique des dîners.

El Cisne de Oro del hotel Hyatt en Gainey Ranch de Scottsdale ofrece un marco apropiado para una cena romántica.

"The Golden Swan" (Der goldene Schwan) im Hyatt in der Gainey Ranch in Scottsdale bietet den geeigneten Rahmen für ein romantisches Abendessen.

スコッツデールのハイアット・リージェンシー・アット・ゲイニー・ランチにあるゴールデン・スワン・レストランではロマンチックなディナーがエンジョイできる。

在斯卡茨得爾(Scottsdale),蓋妮蘭奇(Gainey Ranch)凱悅(Hyatt)飯店的金天鵝餐廳 (Golden Swan),提供高雅的餐具和羅曼蒂克的晚餐。

pages 88-89

Des palaces comme le Scottsdale Princess ont fait du Grand Phoenix une destination de choix pour des touristes du monde entier.

Los hoteles como Scottsdale Princess hacen que Phoenix metropolitano sea la destinación preferida para los visitantes de todo el mundo.

Ferienhotels, wie das Scottsdale Princess machen Phoenix zu einem vorzüglichen Reiseziel für Besucher aus aller Welt.

スコッツデール・プリンセスのようなリゾートが世界中からビジターをフェニックス大都市圏に引きつけている。

度假勝地，如斯卡茨得爾公主飯店(Scottsdale Princess)，使大鳳凰城成為世界遊客的響往勝地。

page 90

Le légendaire hôtel San Marcos a été construit dans les années 20 par le Dr. Alexander Chandler, fondateur de la ville de Chandler.

El legendario hotel de San Marcos fue construido por el Dr. Alexander Chandler, fundador de la ciudad de Chandler.

Das legendäre San Marcos Hotel wurde von Dr. Alexander Chandler, dem Begründer der Stadt Chandler, gebaut.

伝統あるサン・マルコス・リゾートはチャンドラー市の創設者であるアレキサンダー・チャンドラー博士により建設された。

亞歷山大錢德勒博士(Dr. Alexander Chandler)(錢德勒城的創建人）建造了傳奇的山姆馬可士(San Marcos)度假中心。

page 91

L'hôtel Wigwam à Litchfield Park est l'un des "5-étoiles" de la région.

El hotel Wigwam en Litchfield Park es uno de los hoteles de cinco estrellas.

Das Wigwam Hotel in Litchfield ist eines der Fünf-Sterne-Hotels der Gegend.

リッチフィールド・パークにあるウィグワム・リゾートはこの地域にある五ツ星のリゾートの一つである。

位在林屈費爾德公園(Litchfield Park)的維格彎(Wigwam Resort)渡假中心是鄰近五星級度假飯店之一。

page 92

La cascade artificielle du Scottsdale Princess.

La cascada del hotel Scottsdale Princess.

Der Wasserfall im Scottsdale Princess.

スコッデール・プリンセスの滝。

斯卡茨得爾公主飯店(Scottsdale Princess)的瀑布。

page 93

La piscine avec plage de sable du Hyatt à Gainey Ranch.

La piscina de arena de mar del hotel Hyatt en Gainey Ranch.

Der Swimming Pool mit Sandstrand im Hyatt in der Gainey Ranch.

ハイアット・リジェンシー・ゲイニー・ランチのプール脇の砂浜。

蓋妮蘭奇(Gainey Ranch)凱悅(Hyatt)飯店的沙灘泳池。

pages 94-95

Le tournoi Tradition a lieu chaque année sur les deux magnifiques parcours de golf conçus par Jack Nicklaus à Desert Mountain.

Tradition Golf Tournament tiene lugar cada año en dos soberbios campos de golf, diseñados por Jack Nicklaus en Desert Mountain.

Das Tradition Golfturnier findet jedes Jahr auf den beiden vorzüglichen Golfplätzen am Desert Mountain statt, die von Jack Nicklaus entworfen wurden.

デザート・マウンテンはジャック・ニクラウスによるデザイで、トラディション・ゴルフ・トーナメントがこの二箇所のゴルフコースにおいて毎年開催されている。

每年傳統高爾夫錦標賽(Traditional Golf Tournament)在沙漠山(Desert Mountain)兩處傑克尼古拉斯(Jack Nicklaus)所設計的高級高爾夫球場舉行。

page 96

La vente Barrett-Jackson de voitures de collection attire chaque année une foule de passionnés d'automobiles à WestWorld de Scottsdale.

La subasta de automóviles clásicos de Barrett-Jackson atrae cada año miles de aficionados del automóvil a WestWorld de Scottsdale.

Die Barrett-Jackson Autoauktion für Oldtimer bringt jedes Jahr Tausende von Automobilfans zu Westworld in Scottsdale.

バレット・ジャクソン・クラシック・カー・オークションは毎年スコッツデールにあるウェストワールドに多くの自動車ファンを集めている。

每年貝若特傑克森(Barrett-Jackson)古董車拍賣吸引成千上萬的汽車迷光臨斯卡茨得爾(Scottsdale)的衛司特沃德(Westworld)。

page 97

La course de ballons Thunderbird Classic prend son départ également de WestWorld.

La competición de Thunderbird Balloon Classic también se celebra en WestWorld.

Die Thunderbird Balloon Classic findet ebenso in Westworld statt.

サンダーバート・バルーン・クラシック。ウェストワールドで開催される。

雷鳥熱汽球賽(Thunderbird Balloon Classic) 也在衛司特沃德(WestWorld)舉行。

page 98

L'équitation se pratique partout, de la manière la plus décontractée ou la plus élégante.

La equitación puede practicarse casi en todas partes, de una manera casual o sofisticada.

Fast überall kann geritten werden, auf lässige oder elegante Weise.

乗馬はどこでも気楽にできるが、フォーマルにも訓練できる。

你可以在任何地方練習騎馬，不論是自娛或是比賽。

page 99

Cette participante au défilé de Fiesta Bowl représente l'un des nombreux haras de chevaux arabes du Grand Phoenix.

Este participante del desfile de Fiesta Bowl representa a uno de los numeros ranchos de cría de caballos árabes.

Dieser Teilnehmer der Fiesta Bowl Parade vertritt eine der zahlreichen Araberzuchtfarmen in Phoenix.

フィエスタ・ボール・パレードの参加者がフェニックス大都市圏にある数多くのアラビア馬の飼育場を代表している。

這匹參賽者是代表大鳳凰城許多飼養阿拉伯馬牧場參與費思塔遊行的名馬之一。

page 100

L'art est présent dans de nombreux lieux publics, et le cheval en est l'un des thèmes les plus populaires.

El arte esta presente en muchos lugares públicos y los caballos constituyen un tema popular.

Auf vielen öffentlichen Plätzen ist Kunst gegenwärtig und Pferde sind ein beliebtes Thema.

町のいたるところに芸術があり、馬がポピュラーなテーマとして扱われている。

藝術作品在公共場所比比皆是，而馬是受歡迎的主題。

page 101

Les amateurs de Western Art et de Cowboy Art viennent des quatre coins du monde.

Los aficionados del arte del Oeste y de los vaqueros vienen de todas partes del mundo.

Western- und Cowboykunstliebhaber kommen aus aller Welt.

ウェスタンとカーボーイ愛好家達が世界中から集まっている。

西部與牛仔文化藝術愛好者來自世界各地。

pages 102-103

Ce groupe de chevaux en bronze, grandeur nature, de l'artiste Buck McCain, accueille les visiteurs de la Franchise Finance Corporation of America.

El conjunto de caballos de bronce, de tamaño natural, del artista Buck McCain de Arizona, adorna el acceso a Franchise Finance Corporation of America.

Die lebensgrosse Gruppe von Bronzepferden des Arizonakünstlers Buck McCain verziert den Zugang zur Franchise Corporation of America.

アリゾナのアーティスト、バック・マッケイン作による実物大の馬のブロンズ像がフランチャイズ・ファイナンス・コーポレーション・オブ・アメリカの入り口を優雅に飾っている。

亞利桑那州(Arizona)的藝術家伯克麥肯(Buck McCain)捐贈一組與實物一般大小的青銅馬與美國財務公司(Franchise Finance Corporation of America)。

page 104

L'apparition de prestigieux immeubles de bureaux constituent souvent la marque la plus apparente de la vitalité d'une ville.

Prestigiosos edificios de empresas constituyen a menudo una prueba visible de la vitalidad de la comunidad.

Bedeutende Firmengebäude sind oft das sichtbarste Zeichen der Lebenskraft einer Gemeinde.

著名な会社のビルが最も視覚的に地域のバイタリティーを表わしている。

著名公司的建築物通常是一個社區最醒目的標誌。

page 105

Les tours jumelles du Renaissance Center sont une illustration du récent essor économique du Grand Phoenix.

Las torres gemelas del Renaissance Center ilustran el crecimiento económico de Phoenix metropolitano en los recientes años.

Die Zwillingstürme des Renaissance Centers kennzeichen das wirtschaftliche Wachstum von Phoenix in den letzten Jahren.

ルネッサンス・センターのツインタワーが近年のフェニックス大都市圏の経済成長を象徴している。

李蘭聖中心(Renaissance Center's)的雙塔說明了大鳳凰城近年來的經濟發展。

pages 106-107

L'aéroport Sky Harbor International dessert le Grand Phoenix. C'est l'un des plus actifs au monde.

Sky Harbor International sirve a Phoenix metropolitano y es uno de los aeropuertos de más tránsito del mundo.

Der Flughafen Sky Harbor International versorgt Gesamt-Phoenix und zählt zu den verkehrsreichsten Flughäfen der Welt.

スカイハーバー国際空港はフェニックス大都市圏で操業する空港で、世界でも最も発着率が高い空港である。

位於大鳳凰城的思蓋哈伯(Sky Harbor)國際機場是世界上最繁忙的機場之一。

page 108

Représentées par leur logo, ces sociétés sont parmi celles dont le siège est dans le Grand Phoenix.

Representados por sus logotipos, estas corporaciones están entre las que consideran Phoenix metropolitano como su casa.

Diese Firmen, gezeigt durch ihre Logos, nennen Phoenix ihren Heimatsitz.

ロゴによって代表されるように、これらの会社はフェニックス大都市圏を本社としている。

一些大企業都在標語上說明他們以大鳳凰城爲家。

page 109

Des espaces de travail raffinés ajoutent à la manière amicale et décontractée de conduire les affaires dans le sud-ouest américain.

Sofisticados medio ambientes de empresas complementan la manera informal y cordial, típica del suroeste, de hacer negocio.

Anspruchsvolle Firmenanlagen ergänzen die lässige und freundliche Southwestern Art Geschäfte zu machen.

知的なビジネス環境がカジュアルでフレンドリーな米国南西部のビジネス気質とうまく融和している。

多元化的企業環境與輕鬆友善的西南部洽談生意方式相輔相成。

page 110

Des sociétés de dimension internationale contribuent à l'économie locale.

Las grandes corporaciones contribuyen a la economía local.

Bedeutende Firmen tragen zur örtlichen Wirtschaft bei.

主要な会社が地域の経済に貢献している。

主要的企業帶動了當地的經濟成長。

page 111

La Mayo Clinique de Scottsdale est l'un des nombreux équipements médicaux et hospitaliers qui ont contribué à faire de Phoenix un centre important de traitement et de recherche.

Mayo Clinic de Scottsdale está entre muchas de las excelentes facilidades médicas que han hecho de Phoenix metropolitano un centro médico importante.

Die Mayo Klinik in Scottsdale ist eine der vielen medizinischen Einrichtungen die Phoenix zu einem wichtigen Zentrum in der medizinischen Versorgung machen.

メイヨ・クリニック・スコッツデールは傑出した医療施設の一つで、これによりフェニックス大都市圏が主要な医療の中心地域となっている。

杰出醫療設備之一的斯卡茨得爾(Scottsdale)瑪友診所(Mayo Clinic)使大鳳凰城成爲主要醫療中心之一。

page 112

La lumière crée de séduisants effets d'optique dans la façade de verre des bureaux de l'Esplanade.

El sol crea auténticos juegos visuales en las paredes de cristal de los edificios de Esplanade.

Optische Spiele der Sonne in den Glaswänden der Esplanadegebäude.

太陽がエスプラナーデのビルのガラスの壁に視覚的な要素を加えている。

炫麗陽光閃耀在艾思伯内特(Esplanade) 的玻璃牆上。

Note of the author.

Most of the photographs that appear in this book were taken specifically for this purpose, from May, 1994 to June, 1995. I express my gratitude to the residents of Greater Phoenix who never turned their backs to my camera, but contributed smiles most of the time. Many manifested a great interest in this book, thus confirming my feeling that civic pride was strong throughout our Valley of the Sun.

My equipment included three Nikon cameras and a variety of lenses. Films were either Kodachrome or Fuji Provia.

Michel F. Sarda

Index of names

Adler, Stan, 86
Agua Fria, 11
Alsop, John T., 11
All-Arabian Horse Show, 98
America West Airlines, 4, 106, 123
America West Arena, 49
American Graduate School of Intl. Management,
      See also Thunderbird, 4, 57, 129
Amin, Kamal, 4, 59
Anti-Saloon League, 12
Apache, 10
Architecture Magazine, 44
Arizona, 9-14, 16, 21, 22, 25, 28, 33, 42, 54, 58, 65, 66
      72, 111
Arizona Biltmore, 12, 30-31
Arizona Canal, 11-12
Arizona Cardinals, 55
Arizona Center, 44, 45, 84, 104
Arizona Historical Society (& Museum), 28
Arizona State College, 11
Arizona State Teachers College (ASTC), 11
Arizona State University (ASU), 11, 32, 48, 54, 55
      58, 59
Arizona Theatre Company (ATC), 63
Armstrong, John Samuel, 11
ASU, see Arizona State University
ASU West, 58
ASU School of Music, 58
Australia, 7
Avondale, 17
Ballet Arizona, 62
Bank of America, 4, 122
BankOne Center, 104
Barrett-Jackson Classic Car Auction, 96
Bartlett Lake, 77-79
Behn, Harry, 70, 91
Benton, Patricia, 20
Best Western International, 4, 143
Biltmore (see Arizona Biltmore)
Biltmore Fashion Park, 84
Bimson, Walter Reed, 11
Blockbuster Desert Sky Pavilion, 60
Bolton, Herbert, 9
Botanical Garden, 70
Boulders, 14
Bridgewood Press, 136
Bruder, Will, 56-57, 82
Buckeye, 13, 17
Bull HN Information Systems, 4, 120
Bushby, D. Maitland, 22
Cactus League, 52
California Angels, 52
Camelback Mountain, 18, 34, 68
Campos, Father de, 10
Canada, 7, 106
Capitol, 10, 22, 25
Carl Bertelsmann Foundation, 8, 44, 72
CenterPoint, 46, 48
Chandler (City of), 12-13, 16, 90
      Ostrich Festival, 60
Chandler, Dr. Alexander, 12-13, 90
Clark, Ann Nolan, 101
Clark, Badger, 33
Cornoyer-Hedricks Architects, 111
Cosanti (Foundation), 65
Curtis, Philip C., 12, 66

DeMars, James, 62
DeRoy, Mark, 85
Desert Botanical Garden, see Botanical Garden
Desert Mountain, 93-95
Dial Corp, 38, 130
Dixon, Maynard, 68
Duppa, Darrell, 12-13
Durham, G. Homer, 54, 59
El Mirage, 17
Ensign, Bill, 34
Esplanade, 111-112
Evans, Jessie Benton, 26
Falcon field, 13
Fiesta Bowl, 40, 52, 54, 99
Fifth Avenue (Scottsdale), 23
Fleischer, Donna and Morton, 61, 102
Fountain Hills, 17
Fort McDowell, 12-13
Fowler, Benjamin A., 11
Gammage, Dr. Grady, 11
Garrett Aerospace, 14
Gila River Community & Casino, 150-151
Gilbert, 13, 17
Glendale (City of) 8, 12, 16, 48, 58
Golden Swan, 87
Goldstein, David Ira, 63
Goodacre, Glenna, 38
Goodyear, 14, 17
Grady Gammage Auditorium, 59, 60
Great Depression, 13
Greater Phoenix, 7-14, 16, 20, 34, 35, 38, 40, 47, 48,
      52, 58, 60, 67, 72, 84, 87, 98, 99, 102-103,
      106, 111
Greater Phoenix Economic Council, 4, 115
Gross, Christopher, 87
Guadalupe, 42
Guérithault, Vincent, 87
Hall, Sharlot, 19, 26
Hayden, Senator Carl T., 13
Hayden, Charles Trumbull, 11
Hayden Library (ASU), 58
Hayden Milling & Farming Ditch Co.,
Hayden Square, 49
Heard, Dwight & Maie, 28
Heard (Museum), 28, 60
Herberger, Dr. Roy A., 57
Herberger Theater, 44, 60, 63
Heritage Square, 44
Hermosillo, 22
Hohokam, 9, 10, 21
Houser, Alan, 28
Hyatt at Gainey Ranch, 87, 93
Iliff, Warren, 71
Intel, 13-14, 121
Jesuits, 9-10
Junker, John, 54
Jokake Inn, 26
Kino, Padre Eusebio, 9-10, 22
Labrouste, Henri, 57
Lath House, 44
Litchfield, Paul W., 14
Litchfield Park, 14, 17, 91
Luckingham, Bradford, 13-14
Luke Air Force Base, 13-14
Lykes House, 82

Maricopa Community Colleges, 58
Maricopa County, 11-14, 16
Martinez, Julian, 22
Mathiesen, Pat, 62
Mayo Clinic Scottsdale, 14, 111
McCain, Buck, 21, 102
McDonnell Douglas Helicopters, 14, 119
McDowell Mountains, 31, 34, 80
McFarland, Senator Ernest W., 13
McGary, Dave, 101
Mell, Ed, 100
Mesa (City of) 8, 12, 16, 104
      Southwest Museum, 60
Mexico, 9, 20, 114
Mexico City, 7
Mill Avenue, 46, 48, 84
Miller, Robert Bear, 76
Moeur, Governor Benjamin B., 13
Motorola, 13-14
Mormon(s), 12
Morning Star, 43
Mount Olympus, 11
Murphy, William J., 11-13
NAFTA, 57, 106
Native American(s), 8, 21, 28, 32, 43, 60
Navajo, 32, 43, 66
Nelson Fine Arts Center, 58
Neurological Barrows Institute, 14
New Deal, 11, 13
Nicklaus, Jack, 93, 95
Normal School of Teachers, 11
Ormandy, Eugene, 59
Orpheon Theater, 35
Papago, 21
Papago Mountain, 76
Papago Park, 28
Papago Plaza, 85
Parada del Sol, 40
Parks, Bob, 23
Patriot Square, 38
Peoria, 13, 17, 53
Phoenician (Resort), 14, 26
Phoenix (City of) 7-14, 16, 24, 25, 37, 38, 44, 63, 72, 109
      Art Museum, 13, 60
      Central Library, 56, 57
      City Hall, 34, 35, 44
      Museum of Science and Technology, 60
      Symphony Hall, 60
Phoenix Suns, 41, 49, 50-51,
Phoenix Symphony, 13, 62
Phoenix Zoo, 71
Pinnacle Peak, 76
Pima, 9-12
Poling, Charles S., 37, 82
Pope John Paul II, 24
Powell, Lawrence C., 8, 11
Predock, Antoine, 58, 82
Prescott, 11
Pow Wow, 32
Puddle Jumpers, 38
Pueblo Grande, 10
Pumpkinsville, 10
Renaissance Center, 104-105, 109
Ridge, Barbara and Sterling, 58
Rios, Alberto, 62
Roosevelt Dam, 11-12
Roosevelt, President Theodore, 11
Rosson House, 44

Saint Mary's Basilica, 24
Salina, 10
Salt River, 9-11, 21
San Diego Padres, 53
San Marcos Resort, 12, 90
Santa Fe, 9
Santans, 34
Schermer, Beth, 111
Schevill, Margaret E., 81
Scholder, Fritz, 64, 65
Scott, Winfield, 12
Scottsdale (City of) 10, 12-14, 16, 23, 40, 65, 72, 76, 84-85, 87, 100,
      Public Library, 48
Scottsdale Fashion Square, 84
Scottsdale Princess, 14, 87-89, 92-93
Seattle Mariners, 53
Sky Harbor International Airport, 106-107
Smalley, Delos H., 23
Smith, John "Yours Truly", 11
Soleri, Paolo, 65
Sonora, 9, 22
Sonoran desert, 20, 34, 70, 77
South Mountain, 37
Southern Pacific Railroad, 13
Southwest Airlines, 106
Squaw Peak, 68
Squires, Joan H., 62
Sun Devil Stadium, 55
Suncor Development Corp., 116-117
Super Bowl, 55
Surprise, 17
Swilling, Jack, 10-11
Taliesin West, 31
Tempe (City of) 10, 11-14, 16, 42, 46, 48, 49, 76
      City Hall, 48
      Arts Festival, 76
Thunderbird (AGSIM), 57
Thunderbird air base, 13
Thunderbird Balloon Classic, 96
Tolleson, 13, 17
Tokyo, 7
Tradition Golf Tournament, 93
Troon Village, 80
Tucson, 9, 12, 42
United States, 26, 40, 42
Valley National Bank, 13
Valley of the Sun, 9-14, 47, 53
Vandeveer, Vesta H., 74
Verde River, 21
Waddell, John, 44, 67
Wadsworth, Beuylah, 21
Walton, Eda Lou, 67
WestWorld (of Scottsdale), 76, 96
Wetherill, Hilda, 73
Wickenburg, Henry, 10
Wigwam (Resort), 14, 91
Williams AFB, 13
Williams, Governor Jack, 54
Wiltbank, Milo, 5, 80
Wright, Frank Lloyd, 12, 30, 31, 59, 82, 90
Yaqui, 42
Yuma, 11
Zoo, 71